SATAN'S SEVEN SCHEMES

SATAN'S SEVEN SCHEMES

AN OVERCOMER'S GUIDE TO SPIRITUAL WARFARE

Paul deParrie

Wolgemuth & Hyatt, Publishers, Inc.
Brentwood, Tennessee

© 1991 by Paul deParrie. All rights reserved.
Published January 1991. First Edition.
Printed in the United States of America.
97 96 95 94 93 92 91 90   8 7 6 5 4 3 2 1

Unless otherwise noted, all Scripture quotations are from the New American Standard Bible, copyrighted by The Lockman Foundation 1960, 1962, 1963, 1968, 1971, 1972, 1973, 1975, 1977, and are used by permission.

Wolgemuth & Hyatt, Publishers, Inc.
1749 Mallory Lane, Suite 110
Brentwood, Tennessee 37027

Library of Congress Cataloging-in-Publication Data

deParrie, Paul.
    Satan's seven schemes : an overcomer's guide to spiritual warfare
/ Paul deParrie.—1st ed.
        p. cm.
    Includes bibliographical references and index.
    ISBN 1-56121-050-1
    1. Devil. 2. Christian life—1960– 3. Bible. O.T. Genesis III—
Criticism, interpretation, etc. I. Title.
BT981.D47 1991
235′.4—dc20   90-21239
                                                                            CIP

To W. A. Giersdorf,
whom God used
to teach me that
*"God's Word says what it means
and means what it says"*

CONTENTS

ACKNOWLEDGMENTS

I would like to acknowledge the steadfast courage of Dr. Henry Morris, Ken Ham, and all those at the Institute for Creation Research for withstanding the hurricane winds of our time and clinging to the truth of God's Word. I also thank Michael Hyatt for his ministry of encouragement and enthusiastic support.

INTRODUCTION

*"[Satan] is a liar, and the father
of it."*

John 8:44, KJV

L ies and darkness are often synonymous in Scripture.
Both limit a person from knowing and doing right.
And the cure for darkness—at least for those who *want* to
see—is to turn on the light. The same is true for falsehood.
For those who *love* the Truth the cure is the Truth.

Often misquoted is the dictum of Christ that the truth
will make one free; less often noted is the precondition to
that statement, *"If you abide in my word, then you are truly
disciples of mine"* (John 8:31, NAS).

This volume is an attempt to shed a little light on
popular beliefs whose roots are in the forked tongue of
the Serpent of Eden. Satan cannot create, but he may do
two things to deceive us: he may directly contradict Truth
or he may tell a distorted truth. We, his experimental
guinea pigs, may either rebuff his pronouncements, accept them, or allow niggling doubt and indecision to rot
the core of faith.

I believe God has given us the revelation of the book
of Genesis to display the origins of many things, including

1

sin and temptation. Let me make it clear, however, that Genesis is no mere allegory for us to spiritualize or use to seek typology and other arcane understandings. Genesis is *actual history* and nothing less. The last thing I wish to do is to lead anyone into the miry bogs of spiritualized interpretation.

My point is simply that the lies used on Eve are the same ones that are warmed up, rehashed, and served over and over again to a lie-hungry, carnal nature. Millennia of human error and degradation punctuates that success. But I also know that believers can train themselves to spot and avoid these deceptions if they will examine their roots and become familiar with the tactical devices of the devil. As the Apostle Paul once noted, "we are not ignorant of his devices" (2 Corinthians 2:11, KJV). Nor should we be ignorant.

This work is intended to be instructive rather than exhaustive. I will touch on many variants of the Edenic lies without resting for deep analysis and without any vain hope of covering them all. It is my desire to awaken fellow believers to a tool for discernment of the Truth and exposure of satanic trickery.

Jesus warned us, "Take care what you listen to" (Mark 4:24). And we do well to be careful that what we hear is true, measured against God's Word. Remember that Scripture warns, "There is a way which *seems* right to a man, but its end is the way of death" (Proverbs 16:25, emphasis added). Believers, like all others, are still subject to this carnal bent, but knowledge of God's Truth and a dogged insistence on believing it will mortify that propensity for error.

> My son, do not forget my teaching, but let your heart keep my commandments; for length of days and years of life, and peace they will add to you. (Proverbs 3:1–2)

ONE

IN THE BEGINNING
WAS THE LIE

Your face flushes and your ears burn when you remember the time you were lied to—the time you
were *really* taken in.

You can remember it all. You always will. "How could
I have been so stupid?" you ask yourself.

It was partly because of a doctrinal error and partly
the exciting ministry of a well-known preacher that
hooked you. You contributed heavily, bought the books,
records, and tapes, recommended him to friends, and
even dragged several along to the crusade when he came
to town. Some of your friends expressed doubts about
your enthusiastic support for the man, but you would
hear none of it. In any case, the discovery of your deception took a lot of wind out of you. The "preacher" was
discovered in some shady dealings and the whole facade
collapsed.

You wonder why—or how—such a thing as a lie
would even work. But lying is an ancient craft. In fact, it
was the first tool of Satan, and he has had thousands of

years to hone its edge for maximum effectiveness. Lies *work!* They slip into a thought or a conversation on the wings of an assumption and undermine the very ground on which you stand. They appeal to the petty prides and little lusts in us that Satan knows so well. And before you know it, you are bound.

Yes, the sly Serpent knows well how it works. And it started long ago. . . .

ᕔ ᕔ ᕔ

The tree had some unnamed appeal. Eve had been studying it for a few moments, but she felt a sudden chill of wrongness and turned to leave.

"Has God said?" asked a voice smooth, soft, and melodious.

Eve looked back at the Serpent, its scaly skin glistening in the afternoon light.

"Has God said," asked the Serpent, "that you shall not eat of every tree that is in the garden?"

Eve furrowed her brow briefly, then answered confidently, "We may eat of the fruit of all the trees of the garden but the tree in the middle of the garden, God has said, 'You shall not eat of it . . .' " Eve hesitated, her voice faltered. She looked at the ground, then back at the Serpent and added, "or even touch it, or we will die!"

The Serpent's brilliant colors rippled. He spoke as if to a child. "Oh, you surely won't *die.* God knows that if you eat of it, then your eyes will be opened—you will be like gods, knowing good and evil."

Eve fixed her gaze on the fruit. The satiny, supple texture of its skin seemed opaque with an inner glow. She *was* a little hungry. The luster of the fruit seemed to speak to Eve of satisfying a deeper hunger. Hanging there from the tree, the fruit seemed to be the solution to her desire for wisdom.

Eve reached out and touched it. The Serpent's eyes glittered. With a small jerk she snapped the fruit from the stem.

ﮨ ﮨ ﮨ

The rest of the story is known, as are the tragic results. Deception and rebellion against God mar all mankind, as evidenced by man's pitiful attempts to cover his nakedness with perishable works, a legacy of cunning deception and mindless gullibility, and a world full of sin and wickedness that would require nothing less than the horrifying death of God's only-begotten Son to remedy.

In this paradise of God the Serpent, Satan, unleashed his most potent (and some say his only) weapon against God and man—*the lie.* And potent it was—*and is.* Paganism, in all its manifestations, is the result.

Paganism, for our purposes, is any system of beliefs that is designed to exclude God, deny His path of salvation, or worships and serves created things rather than the Creator (see Romans 1:18–23). Serpentine lies are the foundation of all paganism, whether that paganism presents itself as scientific or nihilistic or religious.

Though Satan vainly imagines himself to be God's equal, he falls immeasurably short. For one, Satan is not creative, but his self-delusion in this matter makes his lies especially cunning and dangerous. His lies were successful in the pristine Garden with the perfect, guileless Eve. While his lies are subtle, Satan merely retells endless variations on the same foundational untruths he used on the first woman.

Even today, the same lies prevail where the light of Christ does not shine. And as Paul the apostle urged that we be not ignorant of Satan's devices, we also do well to investigate the nature of Satan's deceit.

Disbanding the Church's Agnostic Club

"I would not have you ignorant," Paul the apostle wrote on several occasions. He would not have us ignorant of spiritual gifts, the mystery of Israel, and the typology of the church, and the fate of those who had died in the Lord, among other things.[1] But a curious interpolation appears later saying that he and his readers were not ignorant of Satan's "devices."[2] Here, Paul refers to a church discipline case and the specific device of planting seeds of unforgiveness and division within the church.

When Paul said he did not want the church ignorant, he used the Greek word *agnoeo*, a word based on *gnosko* or "knowledge" with the *a* before it signifying "no" or "lack of" knowledge. From this Greek word we derive the word *agnostic* which literally means, "I am ignorant" or "I don't know." Paul wanted no *agnostics*—no one ignorant—in the church.

Of course, Paul was the first to warn believers away from knowing too much of the intricacies of the devil's work.[3] In fact, he would agree that it would be foolish to try to know about *every single* demonic doctrine. There are simply too many. But Paul did not—as some do today—advise ignoring enemy tactics in some misguided attempt to have a "positive" faith.

I have read that bank tellers are trained to spot counterfeit money by courses that make them *so* familiar with the real bills that no bogus money will fool them. A similar course has been recommended for Christians—that is, to become so familiar with God's Word that lies would stand out in high relief. I believe this proposal has much merit, and because of this, God also records Satan's tactics in the Garden. He intends that we learn something of the strategy which our enemy is liable to employ. God wants us to be familiar with *all* that He has revealed in Scripture—including how Satan works against God and His people.

Since believers still have to contend with their carnal nature, they cannot depend on the study of the positive truth alone to the exclusion of being aware of the enemy plan to bring their faith to nought. Knowing the truth about our enemy—and our own carnal nature—is necessary. The carnal nature, though counted as dead in Christ's death, still wields enough power to blindside us if we ignore its potential ability to subdue us.

False beliefs have enormous power to bind people— bind from doing God's will, bind from comprehending God, bind from worship, and, ultimately, bind people from salvation itself. If we do not believe God's truth, our whole lives, and the lives of those we touch, will be distorted, damaged, or destroyed. Many things that lie in our minds as "perfectly reasonable" assumptions are founded upon the central untruths of the Serpent in the Garden.

Now is *not* the time for complacent *agnost*-icism inside the church, but rather a rousing of ourselves to the immutable truths of God.

A Challenge at the Foundation

"Has God said?" the Serpent asked first.

At the core of human life is the question of God's believability—not whether or not someone believes *in* God, but whether they can *believe* God! The entire spectrum of human behavior is dependent on what someone actually believes. If they believe what God says, they will act accordingly.

In the Garden, Satan first questioned whether God had actually spoken to Eve. Following this, Satan distorted God's prohibition of the fruit of the Tree of the Knowledge of Good and Evil. He stretched that command to include *all* the trees of the Garden, a typical satanic implication which denies the goodness of God toward us.

Eve naturally recoiled at Satan's distortion of God's command in much the same way that Christians today react to the distorted view nonbelievers have of Christian life. But in Eve's retort she *added* to God's Word in her own way, thus weakening her own spiritual footing. Her stand was partly on fear.

This slick footing of Eve's was of little value when the Serpent) then directly challenged God's Word, saying, "You shall surely not die." Eve may have wondered *why* God would falsely threaten death, but Satan anticipated the question. "God knows," said the slithering snake, "that on the day that you eat thereof your eyes will be opened and you will be as gods—knowing good and evil."

In this apparently short description of the events of the Garden, there are seven central lies that Satan has used for thousands of years to bind, and to blind, people.

1. Hath God said . . . ?

2. You shall not eat of *every* tree in the Garden?

3. You shall surely not die.

4. For God doth know that in the day that you eat thereof . . .

5. Your eyes shall be opened.

6. You shall be as gods.

7. Knowing good and evil.

These seven lies and their many variations will be exposed in the following chapters. This will not be a mere exercise in the spiritualization of Scripture, for I am fully convinced that the temptation in the Garden is *actual history*. But I also believe that God's record of the introduction of sin into His creation serves as a template of satanic deception and a warning against his wiles. The entire Genesis account lays a foundation for the rest of the Bible without which the most important Biblical doctrines become mere whim.

The Human Equation

Meanwhile, back in the Garden the lie was complete. Now Eve stood transfixed before the fruit. Her appetite nudged her forward. It was the prospect of wisdom—godhood—that finally urged her to snap the fruit from the branch before her.

But lest we overburden Eve, we should remember that Scripture tells us that where she was *deceived*, Adam was *disobedient*. Adam made a completely conscious choice.

Yes, the lie was complete—a foundation upon which to erect myriad facades from the recycled original. Satan would use his craft to whisper endless variations of it to the sons of men in the future. First, question God's integrity, then His intentions for good, His ability or willingness to dispense justice, His candor about His desires, His exclusive holiness, His primacy in righteousness, and His hatred of evil.

Feed man the lie that *he* is central in the universe—that *he* is god, *he* has the power, *he* is the solution. Let man echo the prideful declaration of Satan, "I will . . . I will . . . I will!" (see Isaiah 14:12–15).

But Satan is a perverter, not a creator. So he took twisted truth and attached it to lies. Where man felt inadequate to *be* god, Satan simply humanized god. Satan's legions took on the claim of godhood and became capricious, unpredictable, and evil gods. Man seemed more comfortable with gods who were as perverse as he. A man in the right social position could justify any wickedness under cover of the " ill of the gods." Soon man degenerated to worshiping animals, then inanimate objects. This is precisely the pattern of Romans 1:18–32.

The calculated evil of the first millennium after Adam and Eve's expulsion from the Garden drove God to drown wickedness with the Deluge. But it wasn't long after the floodwaters and the wrath abated that the rapidly multiplying population returned to its rebellious ways. In spite of God's command to "scatter throughout the earth," and their recent experience with the Deluge, Nimrod was able to rally the masses to resist God and begin the seed form of ancient Babylon—Babel.

And the rebellion never seems to stop. The same human beings who would never *think* to question the instructions that come with their video player or their microwave instantly bristle with questions about God's instructions on the most important issues in all of life. They would never, as they do with the Bible, suspect that the plain text saying, "Keep your VCR away from wet locations" would mean anything other than what it says—despite the high probability of "translation errors" from the original Japanese. Yet when the Word says "Flee fornication" or "You shall not commit adultery," suddenly there is this virulent controversy as to what *exactly* constitutes fornication or adultery.

But one thing always stood in the way of the Serpent's complete success—the words of God to Adam and Eve

that the seed of the woman would crush the head of the
Serpent, destroying its thoughts as well as its foul, lying
mouth. The Serpent was doomed to fail in the end.

Review

In this chapter we have established several facts:

- Satan's primary weapon is the lie.

- All human beings are subject to deception because of
  their fallen nature.

- Satan is not creative but merely uses variations on the
  lies of Eden.

- It is unwise for Christians to be unaware of Satan's devices.

- While being an accurate account of history, the Genesis temptation story outlines seven basic lies of Satan.

- The first lie of Satan is to question God's Word.

- Men love darkness rather than light and will question
  God's Word more easily than any other pronouncements.

TWO

JUST ONE
QUESTION, EVE

T he trapper must be careful not to startle the prey, and
the Serpent was more subtle than all the beasts of the
field. No bludgeoning with direct statements such as,
"God is lying to you about that fruit" or "You don't need
to obey God." Not for *this* Serpent! Just the crafty appearance of an inquisitive bystander—"Hath God said . . . ?"

Even the *form* of this lie is deceptive. Here, the Serpent
makes no false assertion. He simply asks a question—a
seemingly innocent question, but one which is calculated
to generate doubt. It is even a question that might be
asked by someone who seriously seeks knowledge.

But the crafty snake actually used the query to form the
point of a wedge to admit unbelief. And the question, despite the chapter title, was *not* just one. "Hath *God* said
. . . ?"—Is there a God? came the hidden implication. "Hath
God *said* . . . ?"—Does God speak? the question echoed sub-
liminally. Does God speak to people? Another question
seemed to harmonize, "Hath God said . . . to *you?*"

Deep down, the question was more than a mere seeker's inquiry. The real questions were much more significant—questions about the existence of God, about His care for and involvement in human existence, His willingness to communicate with His creatures on both a corporate *and an individual* basis.

"Hath God Said . . . ?"

Does God talk to *you*?

- Professor to student radical: "Did you have time to call and advise the President on foreign policy today?"

- Businessman to panhandler: "You say that Rockefeller called just to borrow a few million bucks from you and it tapped you out, huh?"

- Pedestrian to a man driving a battered car: "So when are you going to pick up your Rolls Royce from the shop?"

The mocking tone is built in, just as it might be with this variation of the Serpent's question, "Does God talk to *you*?" The first thing that happens to any believer who receives any enlightenment from the Lord is that sarcastic quiz. Often it happens within the church. Whole denominations, protective of their precious dogmas, will often look narrowly upon anyone who says he has heard from God. Worldly queries begin with the word *God* itself. They ask if God even exists to *do* the speaking. And if He is there, does He really communicate with men at all? And, perhaps most of all, why to *you*?

Quite naturally, the world is skeptical. Unbelievers class people who talk to or hear from God as "crazy." More potently, psychiatric diagnostic tools have come to define people who "hear from God" as schizophrenic. Those who simply believe the Bible's pronouncements to be true, even without an experiential "hearing," are viewed as, at best, naive, childish, foolish, and perhaps somewhat retarded. At worst they are presented as narrow, bigoted, repressed (and thus repressive), spiteful, and juvenile (in the nastiest sense of that word). That such worldly suspicion is fueled by serpentine guile becomes evident when the psychiatric literature conveniently ignores spiritists and "channelers" in this denigrating diagnosis. The media—particularly the news media—scathingly ridicule Christians who "listen to God" while, in wide-eyed naiveté, report the sayings of Ramtha[1] or the advice of "ascended masters" who speak through their disciples. Newspapers fill the void of silence from God when they run horoscopes and publish the carnal ramblings of sage, new gods such as Carl Sagan and Dear Abby. Television personalities blather on about listening to "inner voices" without fear of contradiction and even with an expectation of awe. Yet, God's plain and proven Word lies under layers of dust in hotel room drawers.

But the profane treatment of believers is hardly limited to those who blatantly profess unbelief. Even within the church a curious glaze comes over some eyes when believers bring Scripture into a discussion where it seems to be unwanted.

I cannot help but recall the church board meeting I attended regarding an outgoing pastor. Some members were deeply concerned about how to secure the remainder of a very small loan they had made him.[2] The board discussed putting a lien on the poor (and I do mean *poor*) man's house, having him sign an agreement that the first of his estate—should anything happen to him—would go to that debt. They feared, they said, that while *en route* to his next pastorate, the family could all die in an automobile accident. Several other collection methods were also discussed. When the conversation slowed a bit, I asked if I might speak. Given the nod, I stated that I believed that there was a perfect solution in the Word. I mentioned that Luke 6:35 exhorted us to lend "expecting nothing in return" and that it was perhaps best to simply forgive the debt. There was an audible gasp from the assembled churchmen. One woman carefully and quietly said she agreed with me. But once they gathered their composure, the board members proceeded as though the words had never been spoken.

On other occasions I have heard Christian talk-show hosts become defensive and embarrassed when a nonbelieving guest—especially a psychologist—made a patently unbiblical assertion and believing callers refuted the claim with Scripture. It seems that the Ph.D. behind the man's name conferred more authority than mere Bible verses.

When man is faced with the loss of autonomy or prestige or, perhaps, seeing the hope of some gain, the question, "Hath God said . . . ?" seems to be a very effective satanic lie.

The format of a question rather than a statement does not change the fact that it is a lie and is *intended* to deceive. In truth, a question is one of the best ways to introduce a lie to a person, especially a believer. Believers should question Bible teachings coming from men, that is, they should confirm it by the Word of God. But questioning the authority of Scripture itself is beyond the pale.

Still, there is almost an instant questioning that surfaces whenever God's truth is presented. Stop and think for a moment of the last time that, by whatever means,

God communicated some powerful truth to you: the Word opened to you in an uncommon way or you received some insight on a situation that helped you make an important decision or you knew the answer to a request as you prayed for guidance or a clear Bible verse was implanted in your mind just when all seemed to be confusion. Can you recall how difficult it was to *explain* your newfound assurance to others, even believers? And not only to other believers. No sooner were you on firm footing on your decision, then *even your own mind* seemed to ask, "Hath God said . . . ?"

All three enemies—the world, the flesh, and the devil— assault the believer with the question. I can attest to the times when I have been dissuaded from following an initial leading from God by allowing the icy hand of "Hath God said . . . ?" to cloud my vision. How many times have I doubted God's plainly stated promises of faithfulness and tried to find a shortcut to my own provision? How much we are like Abraham and Sarah who hear the word that God will provide an heir *from their own bodies.* We question whether He *really* said what we plainly heard. Recall the words of our risen Lord on the road to Emmaus, "O foolish men and slow of heart to *believe in all* that the prophets have spoken! Was it not necessary for the Christ to suffer these things and to enter into His glory?"[3] Days before, the disciples were ready to seize the kingdom at knifepoint because they could not—would not—believe what Christ clearly stated: that He must *suffer* at the hands of the wicked before coming into His kingdom.[4]

All of these deceptions stood on the question, "Hath God said . . . ?" And, yet, there are even more subtle versions.

Did God Really Say *That?*

Thomas Jefferson sat at his swivel desk facing the sun and worked carefully with the scissors. A slip of fine paper fell from the snipping to the floor. On the paper the words stood out, "Ye must be born again." On top of it fell another bearing the words, "Repent, for the kingdom of heaven is at hand."

When he finally put the scissors down, Jefferson had created his own bible, but it was no longer, in any real sense, the Word of God. But what Jefferson did was not really unique. He merely acted out physically what most people, including Christians, do in their minds. Jefferson removed what he felt was objectionable from God's Word and selected what he felt God had *really* said. Others merely explain away or ignore what makes them uncomfortable. Jefferson at least had the courage of his lack of convictions and literally tossed out what he did not like and published the remnants. In this case "Hath God said . . . ?" questions whether or not the verse, which we did not like anyway, was actually something God said.

Some theologians see no contradiction in this view of the Bible. They purport that the Bible actually supports *all* beliefs. Using the arcane "science" of higher criticism, alleged Christian theologians pick and choose which Scriptures they wish to believe were in the original text— which words Jesus actually spoke and which were interpolations. One such professor of the Old Testament, Walter Brueggeman, said, "The wonderful thing about the Bible is that you can always find a verse on anything— and you can always find a verse that contradicts it."[5]

The result of this version of "Hath God said . . . ?" is a pseudo-Christianity that operates a smorgasbord from Scripture, a believe-what-you-want-as-long-as-you-are-sincere faith. This religious practice can outwardly resemble Christianity but is minus the truth. Others, like Jefferson, can be content to be deists or theists and be responsible only to themselves for their actions, at least until the judgment.

The subversive message here is that somehow God is unable to protect His Word from corruption. Some theologians say that the Bible has been changed or added to through the years. Other say that a cadre of self-interests have deliberately conspired to make the Bible over for their own benefit. No real evidence backs these assertions. Of course, even if these were true and God is unable to protect the integrity of His Word, then He is an awfully small god. If He could not have accomplished that relatively simple task, there is surely no reason to obey Him or fear His judgments. But I stand with Isaiah who said, "Woe to the one who quarrels with his Maker."[6]

Another unfounded theory is that the Bible is nothing more than a collection of tales passed from generation to generation by word of mouth. It is further claimed that Moses and others merely wrote these down in the form in which they heard them. The hidden assumption here is that like the party game, "Telephone," there would be serious changes in the story as it passed from person to person. This atheistic prop has invaded the popular mind with a vengeance. I am aware of one instance where a man said, "Oh, the Bible was just a bunch of stories passed down by word of mouth until King James wrote them down in the 1600s." Once again we see a theory that presents a god so weak that he cannot protect even his own story from distortion—a very different god from the God I know. "Hath God said . . . ?" Hath oral tradition said?

Within societies with oral traditions the recounted histories are notoriously accurate. The "historian" selects an apprentice, a new "living history book," who is very young and drills him for many years. These young people are not tribal storytellers producing entertainment. In reality, they would never succeed as the tribal historian unless the history were learned word for word, nuance for nuance. Their entire training was to *accurately* retell tribal history, not to amuse people around the camp fire. Societies which lean on oral tradition have no written language. Cultures deemphasize oral traditions as soon as they have a written language to replace the practice.

Moses probably did not refer to oral tradition since he had been immersed in a culture that had its own written language. And since he was being groomed for a high government position, Moses probably had mastered several languages in the forty years he lived in Pharaoh's house. Apparently the Hebrew people had some written language as well, since Moses immediately began writing in it—unless, of course, someone wants to suggest that Moses *invented* the entire written form of Hebrew, both script and grammar.

Both the theory of the subtle drift away from the original words of the Bible and the conspiracy theory of change have been substantially dismantled by investigation of the ancient copies of the manuscripts. Still, there is little effect on slowing this satanic falsehood. Both professional histories and popular ramblings endlessly repeat, "Did God really say *that*?"

Did *God* Really Say That?

In what could probably be described as a more hard-line evangelical version of the last segment's question, many American Christians spend time splitting hairs over whether the words of Jesus are more the Word than the words of Paul. Another dodge to escape responsibility is to reject anything that comes from the Old Testament, as if God suddenly metamorphosed when B.C. turned to A.D.

I have even heard believers who were able to escape the implications of New Testament verses in the book of Hebrews. They gave some elaborate explanation of how the words were directed specifically at Jewish believers and that the statements are not applicable to Gentiles.

What a convenient way to say, "Hath God said . . . ?"

Did God Really *Mean* That?

"'Hath God said . . . ?' that homosexuality is wrong? I mean, I *know* all about Sodom and Gomorrah and all that, but was that what God was *really* trying to say?"

Only if you take Him at His Word.

- "From the tree of the knowledge of good and evil you shall not eat." (Genesis 2:17)

- "Every one who looks on a woman to lust for her has committed adultery with her already in his heart." (Matthew 5:28)

- "If your right eye makes you stumble, tear it out, and throw it from you." (Matthew 5:29)

- "Do not lay up for yourselves treasures upon the earth." (Matthew 6:19)

- "Flee fornication." (1 Corinthians 6:18, KJV)

- "Do not get drunk with wine . . . but be filled with the Spirit." (Ephesians 5:18)

- "Pray without ceasing." (1 Thessalonians 5:17)

- "Rescue those being led away to death." (Proverbs 24:11, NIV)

- "You shall not lie with a male as one lies with a female; it is an abomination." (Leviticus 18:22)

"What is God *really* trying to say?" This little sleight-of-word trick is a favorite among artful dodgers (or should I say, sinful dodgers). These are people who wish to retain their claim to Christianity and still justify their pet sin or bypass a difficult passage such as some of the ones above. By this means, for instance, God's wrath over the awful perversity of Sodom and Gomorrah is magically transformed into His merely being upset over their "inhospitality." Such games are rarely played by people who claim no faith at all toward God and His Word. Only professing believers seem willing to try these verbal contortionists' arts.

And why is such a ruse used? Because it completely turns the tables on true Bible-believing Christians. It makes the sin of homosexuality and other sexual perversions disappear and places the guilt on those who believe the Word by identifying them as "inhospitable" to homosexuals and others. This kind of exegesis requires the skills of a Houdini, who, it was said, could escape *anything*. Here the object is to escape the plain meaning of the text. One has to completely ignore the obvious demand of the Sodomites to "know" Lot's guests in a sexual manner and diligently seek an implication that this was simply bad manners to ask for their favors so directly.

Another favorite version of this serpentine sham is the meticulous redefinition of words like *fornication*. Fornication, which is simply defined as sexual activity outside the confines of the marriage bed, has become sexual intercourse between a man and a woman who are not married to each other or have another spouse. This narrowed interpretation almost completely defuses Paul's exhortation to "flee fornication." Where the original word covered everything from masturbation to bestiality, the *new and improved* definition allows unmarried couples to do nearly anything in the sexual realm except have actual intercourse. Such teachings are actually well received in church singles' seminars.[7] These are not in the old nemesis, the *liberal social-gospel churches,* but ones that consider themselves evangelical.

Still others have suggested that fornication does not exist where the two are *planning* to get married.[8]

But sex is not the only pet sin being defended in this way. Along a different line, I have heard Christians defer other obligations by narrowing the focus of a verse to apply only to the exact situation described. A good example I know of was when a church decided to sue a believer who had contracted a job for them. One of the members asked the assembled leadership why they would sue in violation of the dictum not to take a brother to law over a matter.[9] The elders explained that the 1 Corinthians passage did not apply in this particular case. No reason was given as to *why* the application was wrong, but there was a lot of mumbling about this being a "friendly" suit.

Another time, a self-described "evangelical think-tank" called a press conference to publicly denounce anti-abortion rescuers (those who block abortuary doors) and their sin of "violence." No doubt this group of theologians and theoreticians were simply following the admonition in Hezekiah, "If your brother sins against you, call the media."[10] The first that the local rescuers heard of the censure was through the state's largest newspaper. Not one of these theologians and church leaders ever bothered to contact, speak with, or confront the rescuers on their "offense." When asked about this apparent violation of the principles Jesus set down in Matthew 18:15–17, one of the leaders pled that this verse applied only if there was a "personal" offense and slipped neatly off the hook of the plain Word of God.[11]

Narrowing Biblical interpretations is only one means of questioning the Scripture and excusing oneself from responsibility. Yet another is the increasing use of "cultural interpretation."

The confusing thing here is that understanding the culture of Biblical times can assist our understanding of the Bible. For instance, I was better able to understand the panic and the later great rejoicing of the woman who had lost one of ten coins in the parable[12] once I was told of a particular Middle-Eastern custom. In that culture a woman was given a chain of ten coins as a betrothal gift by her future groom. She wore these in her hair until the wedding, but if she lost one of the coins, it was a sign that she was careless or unworthy and the marriage could be cancelled. That is motivation for an all-out search!

However, such cultural interpretations are only to assist our comprehension of the plain teaching of the Word. But the new game of cultural Scripture reading is used to *eliminate God's commands.* Everything, it seems, that contradicts our present, twentieth-century cultural assumptions—from women's roles, to illicit sex, to proper finances—is neatly snipped out, *a la* Jefferson, and dropped onto the "culturally irrelevant" pile.

Subverting Whole Houses

Francis Schaeffer, the late twentieth-century theologian and prophet, spoke of a high ridge in the Swiss Alps with a valley on both sides.

One time I was there when there was snow on the ground along that ridge. The snow was lying there unbroken, a seeming unity. However, that unity was an illusion, for it lay along a great divide; it lay along a watershed. One portion of the snow when it melted would flow into one valley. The snow which lay close beside would flow into another valley when it melted.

Now it just so happens on that particular ridge that the melting snow which flows down one side of that ridge goes into a valley, into a small river, and then down into the Rhine River. The Rhine River then flows on through Germany and the water ends up in the cold waters of the North Sea. The water from the snow that started out so close along that watershed on the other side of the ridge, when it melts, drops off sharply down the ridge into the Rhone valley. This water flows into Lac Leman [Lake Geneva] and then goes down below that into the Rhone River which flows through France and into the warm waters of the Mediterranean.

The snow lies along the watershed, unbroken, as a seeming unity. But when it melts, where it ends in its destinations is literally a thousand miles apart.[13]

To this, Schaeffer likens the church in its divided belief over Biblical inerrancy. Professing Christians may all look like the same church, but their faith in the inviolability of the Word of God will lead them to entirely different conclusions on living and dying. Those who believe in the Bible as the absolute Word of God will conform their culture to their faith. Those who do not believe in the authority of Scripture will conform their faith to their culture. One is the warm Mediterranean; the other, the icy North Sea—a thousand miles apart.

In a recent presentation by the Institute for Creation Research[14] a speaker asked, "If we cannot believe the first five words of the Bible—'In the beginning God created'— how can we possibly put our faith in any of it? If the first five words are wrong, how do we know the rest of it is right?"

To that argument I would add that if *any* of God's Word is wrong (or outdated, or inaccurate, or only applicable to another culture), how do we know which things are right? If God cannot keep a few historical facts straight, we certainly cannot trust Him on more crucial matters.

The story of the Garden itself is a prime example. It is either true, or God neglected to tell us that it was an allegory, which means that millions of people, including Jesus, have been granting historical credence to a fable. That is, until Charles Darwin was able to rescue us from our horrible deception. Yet, God continues to speak of Adam and Eve throughout Scripture as specially created, distinct individuals who fell as a result of temptation and marred the human character for all their descendants. Is He deceived?

Our unwillingness to believe even plain statements of the Word has subverted the whole house of the church. The mire in which we sink comes primarily from our willingness to add human doubt to the question, "Hath God said . . . ?"

Pin the Blame on the Donkey

Probably the oldest—and sometimes most honored— human trait is for a man to escape blame even after he discovers he is wrong. Certainly our first parents became instant masters of the craft. "The *woman*," cried Adam. "The woman which *You* gave me . . ."

"E-e-k, the snake, Lord," Eve squealed. "That sneaky snake."[15]

Only the Serpent made no excuse.

On another Biblical occasion an erring prophet blamed his unfortunate reapings on his faithful donkey and beat the poor animal.[16]

Israel's King Saul repeatedly excused his rash behavior by blaming others, so this is not a new development in humanity.

In fact, one could say that much of the blame for our condition (in the matter of not knowing God's Word) rests on the great American dependence on experts. We listen too much to what theologians, theoreticians, pastors, and, yes, even book writers *tell us* that the Word means. But the problem is really our own laziness. We don't read the Word for ourselves. We delegate the responsibility of studying to our pastors and others. Even when we detect error in our spiritual leaders, we look the other way. Jeremiah 5:31 says, "The prophets prophesy falsely, and the priests rule on their own authority; *and My people love it so!*" (emphasis added).

I have a friend who once told me that he enjoyed listening to some of the guest preachers who often came to his church, but that he never bought their books. I asked why and he said, "I figure they get all that great stuff from the Bible anyway, and I've *got* one of those."

Would to God more Christians felt this way!

Am I saying, "Don't read Christian books or listen to theologians"? Certainly not! I *am* saying that believers are responsible to verify the teachings of others against the Bible.

In our carnal laziness, however, we have improperly shifted our responsibility to seek and know God's Truth. And since we do not know the Word ourselves, we easily fall prey to the ulterior exegesis of others and even the antibiblical pronouncements of heathen "experts" when they intone, "Hath God said . . . ?"

I have long asserted that God's Word was written for the understanding of *ordinary* people. I do not contend that Bible scholars have nothing to show us at all, but that the Spirit is given to each and every believer so that *all* might be scholars of His Word.

Jesus tells us:

> But when He, the Spirit of truth, comes, He will guide you into all the truth; for He will not speak on His own initiative, but whatever He hears, He will speak; and He will disclose to you what is to come. He will glorify Me; for He shall take of Mine, and disclose it to you. All things that the Father has are Mine; therefore I said, that He takes of Mine, and will disclose it to you.[17]

Studies in the Greek may deepen our appreciation for a particular truth, but that truth will be plainly displayed in the text elsewhere. Typologies, numerical oddities, allegories, and original language wordplays add tremendous interest to Scripture study and cause us to marvel at God's ingenuity. Yet none of these replaces or alters the plainly stated truths of the Word of God.

The Scriptures must be honored in our lives to the degree that no expert, no theologian, no scientist, no psychologist, no government decree that contradicts it will be regarded. None of these should be acknowledged when they say, "Hath God said . . . ?"

Review

In reviewing this chapter we can see that "Hath God said . . . ?" can be rendered as:

- Questioning God's existence.
- Questioning if God speaks at all.
- Questioning if God involves Himself in the affairs of men.
- Questioning if God speaks to individuals.

- Questioning the inerrancy of the Word of God.
- Questioning if God can keep His Word intact.
- Questioning if the Word can be taken at face value.

THREE

THE ALTERED WORD

T he Bible actively discourages sexual expression of
any kind except . . . for procreation only. Even that is
barely tolerated," Michael Pearce was reported to have
said. The columnist trotted out Pearce's words of expert
testimony about Christian morality. What the writer did
not say was that Pearce is an atheist—the leader of a "freedom *from* religion" group.[1] That fact places some doubt on
this particular interpretation of Christian teaching. The
source of the recounted Word of God makes *all* the difference. Of course, due to the columnist's oversight, the readers did not *know* that the quote came from a devout
anti-Christian.

Neither did Eve necessarily know that the Serpent was
God's sworn enemy. As I suggested in the last chapter, it
is possible that the initial question was framed as if it
were from an ardent seeker of Truth. But the troublesome
query, "Hath God said . . . ?" was followed by, "You shall
not eat from any tree of the garden?" Now Eve may have
regarded with suspicion any bald-faced assertion that God
was lying, but the subtle Serpent followed the doubt he
cast on God's command by repeating His dictum back in

31

exaggerated, perverted form. Where God had freed Adam
and Eve to eat of every tree save one, Satan's warped re-
counting prohibited eating from *any* trees.

As anybody can see, this was, like Pearce's quote above,
a complete distortion of God's actual command, and Eve
dove in to set things right. Eve's mistake in her vehement
defense of God's actual words, on the other hand, was to
overcompensate by adding to God's command.

Perhaps I am wrong in attributing this defensiveness
to Eve. The temptation could have been more direct.
Eve's suggestibility could have been higher and the serpentine implication could have been more like, "Who is
this God, anyway, who tells you what to eat and what not
to eat? Does He know what He's talking about?"

The Bible does not tell us Eve's frame of mind. I think
this omission is deliberate because, like the question of the
previous chapter, it can be rendered in a variety of ways
to suit the mental state of the hearer.

Truly, this second question has a number of hidden
reefs. The first shoal is that while it is framed as a question, it could be used as a blunt statement. I would venture to say that every single reader has heard this very
temptation either as a hint of sarcasm or as a blatant taunt.

Exaltation of the Prude God

"I don't want to be a Christian! At least not *yet*," came the
aching whine of the teenage girl.

She may as well have come right out with it—"I want
to go out and have fun while I am young, *then* shrivel up
and become a Christian." Behind that cry lies one of the
most successful lies of the Serpent: You can't be a godly
believer and enjoy life. When you become a Christian,

God drains out all the hormones and you go into a state of emotional and mental torpor.

Meanwhile, Jesus says, "I came that they might have life, and might have it abundantly."[2]

The evidence shows that the abundance of possessions does not make life more satisfying—quite the reverse in many cases (see Luke 12:15). Yet the persistent lie of Satan is that the prohibitions of Scripture are designed to deprive us of all good things. Often this is done through distorting the commands of Scripture to make it appear that the Bible forbids *all* things pleasurable. For instance, libertine groups such as feminists will interpret the Garden Serpent as an analogy for sex and claim that believers see this "tale" as a condemnation of sex itself.

This is precisely why the term *puritan* suffers from an almost universal and false mental picture of a strict, humorless, unkind, sexless, black-and-white clothed Bible-toter. "Has God said that you shall not eat of *any* of the trees of the Garden? Has God said that you shall do nothing enjoyable?"

Satan loves to portray the Christian life as restricted by pointing out the things you cannot do. As a testimony to the effectiveness of this demonic deception, the territory of sin is in most minds defined as "freedom." The world has been completely sold on the idea. Even Christians judge their "freedom in Christ" by how close to sin they can come without getting in trouble, rather than how close to God they can become.

A revelation of the true awfulness and danger of sin seems required for most people to escape the hypnotic power of that false definition. I recall my first few years as a believer. I came out of the hedonistic, drugged-out hippie subculture of the 1960s. Whenever I thought back, I would recall the "good times" that I had while living in

sin. Only with effort I would remember the hours of lone-
liness, fear, depression, and desperation that were between the momentary flashes of "fun." As a tool for the
survival of my faith I learned to cultivate the memories of
the misery that characterized the majority of the time during those years. The propensity of human nature to believe all the "good" about sin is difficult to overcome. But
the whole process is simpler if one just believes God: "The
wages of sin is death" (Romans 6:23).

Sometimes the wages of getting even *close* to sin is
death. "Let a man meet a bear robbed of her cubs, rather
than a fool in his folly" (Proverbs 17:12).

God *hates* sin. And as His children, we must reject the
notion that it is liberating to edge up close to it.

Now I Ask You, Is That *Fair?*

"No one comes to the Father but through Me," Jesus said
(John 14:6). Immediately someone whines, "What about
the native way out in the jungle who has never heard
about Jesus?"

One of the ways that people try to escape responsibility to the Word of God is to judge the "offending" verse
as somehow unfair. The Serpent's words can easily be
read, "Is it really fair for God to put all these trees before
your eyes, give you an appetite for fruit, and command
you not to eat? Would a God of *love* do that?" Here, God's
love and care for His creation is directly challenged. This
temptation is reverberated in a multitude of ways today.
One favorite is, "If God is a loving God, why is there so
much suffering?"

Most often this insidious lie is used to lever someone
toward sin. "Why would God give you a strong natural

desire for sex and tell you that you could not have it? Would that be fair?"

The great pride of this temptation is that it sets up human judgment over God's Word. Our human sense of fairness, which is just as fallen as the rest of us, becomes the plumbline against which all things that *God* says or does are measured. But any casual look at the barbaric history of humanity, especially our century, clearly reveals that we are in no position to judge God. Yet, God is judged by mere human beings. Tragically, this very monstrous pride is displayed by professing Christians in the media. An excellent example was visible when the state of Florida was going to execute the convicted serial killer, Ted Bundy, in 1989. Clergymen were interviewed who flatly stated that they knew that God had commanded the death penalty in the Old Testament, but that *their own compassion* moved them to oppose the execution. The stunning implication is, "Yeah, God is *supposed* to be compassionate, but my compassion is greater"—a sort of more-loving-than-thou attitude toward God.

This is perhaps the most bizarre aspect of this temptation in the Garden. The Serpent both appeals to God's Word and implies rejection of it simultaneously. He quotes it for authority and misquotes it for effect—a clever and effective ploy which still yields returns. Tampering with Scripture is a favorite tool of paganism. Satan recognizes the innate authority of God's Word and tries to bring it into his service. His use of Scripture in the temptations of Christ is a classic example and clear evidence that Satan's devices need not be successful if we submit to God and resist temptation. Most people, however, find it much more convenient to believe the Bible selectively.

These people, whether believers or not, are very picky about the Scriptures. They choose to believe that Jesus said to the woman caught in adultery, "Neither do I condemn you." But they refuse to accept the words that follow them, "Go your way and sin no more," as the true words of Jesus. They love to intone, "Judge not, lest you be judged" and conveniently overlook Jesus' final step of disfellowship for an unrepentant, erring believer.[3] Even the most stark atheists or self-proclaimed pagans will quote the Bible to support their looniest assertions and instantly reject that very Book the moment someone quotes a verse that condemns their activities. "Judge not," they respond from the Bible in answer to convicting quotes given to them from the Bible. It is even more ironic that occultic practitioners—astrologers, channelers, visualizers, and reincarnationists—will use select verses from the Bible to justify their practices, yet they completely reject any of the Word's plain teachings against their wicked works.

Was Satan implying to Eve that *he* was more fair than God? The text doesn't tell us, but we can certainly see that this type of temptation carries that sentiment today—the underlying belief that you will be getting a better deal if you leave God behind and follow the Serpent's suggestions. In the first place, the Serpent gives *suggestions,* with God you get *commandments.* With the devil you will get freedom where God gives restrictions; with Satan you do your own thing, but God demands discipline; away from God you can use your own intelligence to choose between good and evil, but with Him you must submit to His judgment in these matters.

This is humanism at its core: I know what is best for me!

Naturally, all of history reflects the disastrous results of degenerate man's refusal to believe that God's judgments are true and righteous altogether. Every temptation that questions God's goodness toward His people and His good intentions toward the whole world is a satanic lie.

Every temptation that implies that God is unfair, unjust, or that He is "not in touch with reality" is an appeal for you to set yourself up as a judge of God and His Word.

First comes a denial of the Scripture as inerrant or even relevant. Then Scripture, whether added to or subtracted from (see Revelation 22:18–19), is used to undergird false teaching.

A Slip of the Lip

"Neither shall you *touch* it," added Eve.

It may have seemed wise and prudent to Eve to add that extra prohibition. After all, if one did not *touch* the fruit, one would certainly not eat it. There is an element of good sense in this idea. There is only one problem: *It alters God's Word.*

And what is ironic is that it alters God's Word in the very same way the Serpent did—it makes God's command *more restrictive.* To me, this shows that Eve may have already begun to fall; she had already given in slightly to the serpentine line.

Am I saying that it would have been *wrong* for Eve to decide to never touch the fruit? Not at all. God has no objections if you restrict your activities *more* than His Word demands. Paul the apostle makes this clear in his discourse on meat-eating versus vegetarianism.[4] Neither practice, he asserts, makes one more spiritual. Most often, a self-imposed restriction was for the benefit of the individual in overcoming a particular weakness for sin. Today, in the same spirit, former drunkards completely eschew alcohol because of the battle they have with that weakness. The drinking of alcohol is nowhere forbidden in Scripture (save for Nazirites), but this choice by the former drunkard is completely scriptural. In other cases, the restriction is for the benefit of an onlooker's conscience.

There are, however, two dangers with such an answer as Eve's. The first is, as in Eve's remark, the presentation of the additional restriction as *God's command*. The second would be any implication that the added stringency will produce or induce spirituality.

The first error is often an extension of the same zeal and good sense that keeps the former drunkard away from all alcohol. But the pitfall to this is that the Word of God is disparaged because of the excess. There are many examples of this in history. Many years ago, for instance, some churches banned *all* dancing in an effort to help young people quell their temptations toward lust. The absolute prohibition was presented as a mandate of Scripture. The problem arose later when this position was proved to be nonscriptural. However, the carryings-on of anti-dancing preachers are still used today to convince people, particularly the young, that Christianity is a killjoy religion. Bitter fruit, if you ask me. By improper use of God's Word, even for the best motives, we may subvert the actual work of the Spirit in leading souls to Christ.

A more current example of this kind of overreaction is the debate over rock music. There are whole ministries based on teaching that rock music (in the 1800s it was Barbershop Quartets) is "of the devil." I heard a tape by one that claimed it was the syncopated beat itself that defined which music was evil. This position is particularly hard to substantiate, especially since in my understanding many of the psalms of the Bible are written to be played with a syncopated beat. Be that as it may, the Bible itself says nothing about styles of music or types of beats, nor does it make an issue of which musical forms are acceptable to God and which are not. Still, these "ministries" have insisted on a purge of all rock-like music even if it contains Biblically sound lyrics. Yet, I have heard some of the most self-centered "Christian" music performed in the more generally accepted styles.

Outright falsehoods have been perpetrated to float the anti-rock teaching. One tale that has circulated for decades has a missionary's son listening to rock music on his cassette player (it was a phonograph in the 1950s and 1960s) when a native convert informs the missionary that the music is exactly the same as what the witch doctor uses to call up evil spirits. All attempts to verify the tale lead to dead ends—and rightly so. It never happened!

What effect do you think that kind of hyperbole and deception has on the integrity of God's name?

Other groups have proposed that all television, radio, makeup, red dresses, saxophones, or whatever are evil. All of it is a case of confusing evil use of an object with the object itself. This affords Satan with the opportunity to ask, "Hath God said, 'You shall not dance, drink, smoke, listen to rock music, wear makeup, watch television, have sex before marriage, use drugs, or anything else that is fun?' "

The confused and tempted respondent says, "Well, yes, that's true" and often succumbs.

Notice in this temptation that the devil has lumped together the overheated cultural reactions of religionists against dancing and such with genuine sins listed in the Bible. The assumption here is that all of the prohibitions are equally unrealistic. "The preacher says not to dance and not to have sex outside marriage," the Tempter cajoles. "He was *wrong* about dancing. . . ."

The rest is human nature. The carnal nature *wants* to find reasons to sin, so the conclusion is foregone. In the same way, the very act of adding to God's Word put Eve

in the position to fall. Similarly, when we overreact to
Satan's temptation, we set up the entire church for a fall.

But overrestriction is not the only reaction that undermines the power of the Word. We can just as easily respond to the Serpent's assertion that God prohibits too
much by arguing that God allows more than His Word
actually permits. This is the corollary to the error made
by Eve.

In modern times the accusation of restrictiveness in
Christianity has brought about a call to "lighten the ship"
by tossing everything overboard, including the rudder
and the navigational maps and tools.

When the temptation arose, "Hath God said, 'You
shall *never* divorce? (or use birth control or experience sex
outside of marriage?)' " some church leaders became embarrassed by the quaint and arcane commands for com-
mitment, sacrifice, purity, and obedience found in the
Bible. Fearing that they might not fit in with the "modern
understanding of man" (i.e., humanistic psychology),
theologians and popular teachers trampled over one another to become more-with-it-than-thou.

This, too, has served to undermine the power of the
Word and helped sell this lie of the Garden Serpent within
the church.

The Appearance of Wisdom

The second danger of interpolations of God's Word is
how the addendums take on a redemptive power—a
power exclusively reserved to the cross of Christ and the
grace of God. Centuries ago misguided believers voluntarily inflicted pains and discomforts upon their bodies as
payment for their sins. Self-whippings, the wearing of

hairshirts, and deliberate poverty were thought to "mortify the flesh and its desires" when, in fact, they merely served to bloat the spiritual pride of the mendicant.

Jesus had no end of problems with people who made their spiritual points by following rules they had added to God's Word. In fact most of them were able to find justification for disobeying God's actual commandment because they were sticklers on these added regulations. "Neglecting the commandment of God," He said to them, "you hold to the tradition of men. . . . You nicely set aside the commandment of God in order to keep your tradition."[5]

Paul the apostle addressed this very problem in Colossians 2:23—"These are matters which have, to be sure, the appearance of wisdom in self-made religion and self-abasement and severe treatment of the body, but *are of no value against fleshly indulgence*" (emphasis added).

Similar claims of enhanced spirituality are often made by vegetarians who claim that "animal flesh" in the system puts a damper on spiritual growth.[6] The Bible begs to differ. Spiritual growth is a product of the work of the Spirit of God, not what we eat. Jesus plainly states, "Do you not see that whatever goes into the man from outside cannot defile him; because it does not go into his heart, but into his stomach, and is eliminated? Thus He declared all foods clean."[7] Teachings of works-generated spirituality are not Biblical. "He who eats, does so for the Lord, for he gives thanks to God; and he who eats not, for the Lord he does not eat, and give thanks to God," Paul reminds us.[8]

Another manifestation of adding to God's Word had its roots in the hippie movement of the 1960s. Many believers bit into the temptation that "natural" things, as opposed to synthetic, were conducive to spirituality. Many Christians sought to move away from the cities (which were designated as inherently evil) and to the countryside (which was deigned to contain some spiritual element missing in the cities). Others adopted health fads.

Leaning heavily on misused verses like "Your body is the temple of the Holy Spirit" (see 1 Corinthians 3:16; 6:19) and nonbiblical truisms such as "You are what you eat," sincere Christians have ridden every health food and exercise craze to its extreme. From eating plankton and algae to aerobic dancing, from megavitamins to weight-lifting, believers have devoted themselves to spirituality through lean-and-mean bodies. Despite the plain statement of Scripture that "bodily discipline is only of little profit" (see 1 Timothy 4:7–8), many Christians still put more time and effort into planning their wholistic diets or jogging in their seventy dollar Nike™ shoes than to Bible study or ministering to the needs of others. Money is lavished on pricey "health" foods while others in their church survive on rations of food stamps. Christian businessmen merchandise the self-centeredness by sanctifying their offerings with Scripture. As perhaps the grossest example to my knowledge, there was a "Christian" aerobics album promoting increased devotion to Christ while *simultaneously* achieving slim hips and trim thighs. The album cover solemnly intoned, "He must increase, and I must decrease." Yuck!

Then there are the back-to-nature Christians who believe that ideal worship is more proper or possible in natural scenery, as though God had more difficulty reaching the slums of New York than some unspoiled vale in the Rockies. Of course, those who feel that worship is more possible or proper in a beautiful building fall into the same trap. It is a good thing Paul didn't think that way while in the Philippian jail or he would not have carried on so loudly with hymns and praises. Or perhaps Paul sang so loudly only because he knew his voice would have to escape the dank and dingy confines of the prison in order for God to hear him?

The point is that God can work on or with anyone He chooses. I have no doubt that life is more simple and pleasant when one's health is good, but God often uses the weak to perform His greatest work. Think of Paul the apostle: If he exercised, it was in walking to the next town to preach (after being stoned and left for dead) and you never heard him whine about needing a vacation so he would be "more fit to minister." If he ate no meat, it was purely to help him win another soul to Christ. Vegetarianism (naturalism, self-abasement) is nothing, and meat-eating is nothing, but what matters is the *keeping of the commandments of God*, not somebody's list of addendums or traditions.

Review

The second lie, "Hath God said, 'You shall not eat of any tree in the garden?' " can be rendered as:

- Adding to or distorting God's commands.
- Questioning the rightness or fairness of God's commands.
- Questioning the veracity of God's Word.

FOUR

THE DISSOLUTION
OF DEATH AND
JUDGMENT

Y ou can almost hear the "Aw, c'mon!" in front of
Satan's, "You will not die!" as though he were saying, "You won't get caught" or "There are no consequences." Much more than a mere denial of death, this lie
was a denial of God's righteous judgment, of the reality of
consequences for sin. Implicit in that denial is the rejection
of God's justice, His holiness, and His lordship.

Over the years this insidious lie has taken forms from
reincarnation, to the atheist's claim, "When you're dead—
you're *dead!*"; from the Jehovah's Witness idea of reward
for the righteous and final annihilation for others, to those
who see God as incapable of condemning *anyone* to hell.

Feminist, goddess worshiper, and writer, Barbara G.
Walker, points out that even after Adam ate of the fruit,
he lived for over 900 years—he did not die immediately.
"The serpent told Eve the truth," she asserts, "that the
fruit wasn't deadly after all."[1]

One New Age mentor, Leonard Orr, is quoted as saying, "The body is divine—designed to live forever. It is the certainty that you will die that brings your death. Your thoughts are creative."[2] The teaching here is that it is merely your lack of knowledge that causes you to die. Since we are god, the author argues, and one of god's qualities is ever-expanding life, then we should strive to partake of it. The seeds of the teaching are found, they claim, in books like *The Power of Positive Thinking* by Norman Vincent Peale, a professed Christian minister. But the more obvious version is taught by Ramtha, a thirty-five thousand-year-old warrior (a demon spirit), who allegedly speaks through a Washington state woman named J. Z. Knight.

In Western countries, many people have expressed a belief in reincarnation *in spite of claiming that they are Christians.* Neognostics claim that the "truth" of reincarnation was systematically removed from the teachings of Jesus. One writer claims that in the Western Hemisphere "reincarnation was buried alive more than fourteen centuries ago. The conspiring undertakers were the church and state, fearful that their authority could be challenged by a doctrine that made individuals responsible for their own salvation."[3]

"The only judgment on 'the other side' is your own," proclaims the ad for the Raymond Moody books detailing the experiences of those who "died" and returned to life.[4] One of the book jackets describes all the death experiences as "overwhelmingly positive." This denial of death and the judgment is so popular that there are "Christian" versions which also tout the "overwhelmingly positive" death experiences. Indeed, Moody himself laces his presentation liberally with Bible quotes, some in a curious apposition to his emphasis on positive experiences, such as a quote from Daniel 12:2 saying some would have a resurrection of "disgrace and everlasting contempt." Elisabeth Kubler-Ross, leader of the hospice movement and Unitarian, once assured a television audience that even Hitler would be in heaven.

In any case, God is either unwilling or unable to judge His creation. God has to lose all His real personality and become "all things" or "part of all things" to carry off this indifferent, powerless godhood.

The Life Wish

Death may best be defined in terms of separation. Physical death is the separation of the body from its source of life—the soul and spirit—while spiritual death is the human spirit's final separation from its source of life— God. The fact is that Adam *did* die the day he ate of the fruit—he became separated from God the instant he bit and he *knew* it. It took about nine hundred years for his body to catch up completely, but it began to die that day. And since then death has been the rule. Enoch and Elijah were the only known exceptions. Death is still the central reality of a sinful world.

Sin = Death. Period.

But man still retains his creation heritage of the image of God. Herein lies the conflict: Man wants to be what God intended, but he himself has made it impossible because of sin. His every striving to accomplish his God-given destiny is perverted by his sinful nature. One of the deep desires in man is a desire for eternal life. I believe this is what Ecclesiastes 3:11 may be referring to when it says that God has "also set eternity in [man's] heart." Perhaps this is why so few people understand their physical

mortality and why so many, even when terminally dis-
eased, resist admitting the possibility of death.

So the lure of eternal life dangles enticingly before
man's eyes. He looks for escape, but as carnal creatures
are wont, he seeks everywhere but the true source of life.
And in his headlong search he is liable to believe any ridiculous report, follow any ludicrous lead, and face incal-
culable inconsistencies to find physical immortality. Recall
Ponce DeLeon's search for the Fountain of Youth as well
as the fabled quest for the Holy Grail.[5]

Leonard Orr, quoted earlier in the chapter, apparently
believes that anyone can *think* his way to immortality. I
wonder what he makes of Jesus statement, "Which of you
by taking thought can add one cubit unto his stature?"[6]
The whole thing is a rather boneheaded approach. The
Bible is quite plain. As it has been pointed out by others,
we will all have eternal *existence;* the difference is whether
it will be eternal *zoe,* life as God has it, or eternal *thanakos,*
death.

Most people, however, are not quite so dogmatic in
their quest as Leonard Orr. They are aware of a singular
and overwhelming piece of evidence: *Everybody dies!* Physically, at least. So most people need some other approach
to immortality.

Spiritual Ecology—The Recycling of Souls

Ruth Montgomery, so-called Herald of the New Age, lives
and teaches according to her belief that "there truly is no
death."[7] However, her deathless universe is not that of
Leonard Orr but the borrowed, hand-me-down "You shall
surely not die" of ancient, degenerate Hinduism—reincarnation. In this fantasy you do not ever die, you simply get

repeatedly regurgitated into new containers for eternity or until you attain "true enlightenment"—whichever comes first.

Reincarnation, many are surprised to learn, is an *evolutionary* theory. It presumes that things—in this case, beings—continually evolve toward better and better manifestations. This is a reversal of the obvious facts seen in the entropy of all matter as well as the Bible's teaching of the degeneracy of man. Reincarnation does not eliminate death as an event, but seeks to transform it into a (to use the current vernacular) growth experience. And while most forms of the belief carry a kind of judgment for evil under the teaching of karma, this is hardly sufficient replacement for the real judgment of God. It would be difficult to imagine some heinous historical person like Adolf Hitler standing shoulder to shoulder with Paul the apostle in the kingdom of God, but with reincarnation the being who once was incarnated as Hitler will do just that. So much for the justice of God.

The other problem presented by this odious teaching is that there is no implicit standard of morality, and even if there were, how would one know from one life to the next which wrongs he had to amend or avoid from his last life?

And what of the sacrifice of Christ? It is worthless, because each man earns his salvation through correcting his karma. As the Apostle Paul has shown us, if Christ did not die and raise from the dead then we are all lost—there is no grace, no salvation, no resurrection from the dead, and no eternity with Jesus Christ. Acceptance of reincarnation is patent rejection of the gospel. Yet, in America there is a large group of professing Christians who have believed this version of "You shall surely not die!"

The Void at Trail's End

Eastern religions teach that at the end of one's reincarnations, one melds into the great unconscious void, called Brahmin, Nirvana, or the Dow. Here, they say, everyone becomes individually unconscious, one with nothingness.

Western nonbiblical beliefs, on the other hand, dismiss reincarnation altogether and go straight to the void. For atheists, their denial of God extends to their denial of any judgment at all, though I have met atheists who believe in karma and reincarnation.[8] But in the case of total denial of judgment, the "You shall surely not die" reads more like "You shall surely die but you shall not pay for your sins" or "When you're dead, you're dead!"

Others, such as the Jehovah's Witnesses, present a paradise which some may earn by good works (the best of which being to join their group) but consign the mass of humanity to the common grave. By a gross misappropriation of Scripture, such people choose to overlook the justice required by God's very character. They proclaim that God will reward the righteous but will allow the wicked to pass into a nothingness no different from that of the Hindu or atheist. In this doctrine God does not seek justice, and the atheist is right, at least for his own case, "When you're dead, you're dead."

Some religious elements will drone on about the dead having "gone on to a better world" as if there were no hell. This kind of sanctified expunging of God's righteousness and judgment does not produce the brutal spiritual aloneness of the atheist position, the cynical and hopeless rigor demanded by the one-man-god antideist. The calm metaphysical serenity of the better-world-beyond set merely lulls the remaining fragments of guilt and conviction to sleep and allows the "believer" to slip ever so placidly from this mortal coil into hell's inferno.

Whether the lie claims there is no afterlife or that there is an afterlife but no damnation, the falsehood is one and the results are one.

No-Fault Assurance

"He says to himself, 'God has forgotten; He has hidden his face; He will never see it' " (Psalms 10:11). The "he" who says this is "the wicked [who] boasts of his heart's desire." "He" is one who curses and spurns the Lord, who is haughty, and thinks there is no God. "He" is full of deceit, oppression, and he lurks in hiding places to kill the innocent, the afflicted, and the unfortunate (see vv. 3–10).

Nice company, huh? And yet, when *anyone* buys Satan's lie that God's judgment will slumber or sleep, they stand beside him. It is easy to see how the local arrogant humanist may fit the descriptions above, but it is often more difficult to see how a believer could. However, when believers begin to deny God's righteous anger and holy judgment, they set the stage for the reckless behavior and prideful self-appraisals that describe this wicked man of Psalms.

God's very nature *demands* righteous justice and lawful mercy; He could not exist outside of these characteristics. The atheist and the agnostic vehemently deny God and His justice. They are forever frustrated by the lack of justice in the world, but they deny the very Source of justice itself, as well as the Source of the very concept of justice.

I remember working with a very intelligent man who was also an atheist. One morning over coffee he was fuming about a television report he had seen the night before

on the infamous Nazi experimenter, Dr. Mengele, who
had brutally used Jewish men, women, and children in his
heartless tests. Though the man was then thought to be
finally dead, my friend felt deep frustration at the unfin-
ished business of just retribution for Mengele. I told my
friend, "He has not escaped."

For this comment I received the most puzzled expression. Then a look of understanding filled his face followed
by a return to frustration. "I wish I could believe that," he
said with all seriousness.

Obviously, he had failed to see the connection. If you
deny the existence of God, you deny the existence of justice. You cannot have justice without a supreme standard
of justice. Conversely, if you deny justice, you deny God.
Without justice God's character is impugned.

Yet, I have sat in evangelical churches and been told
directly that God does not punish His own people. Even
the loss of rewards for disobedient believers is characterized as "not a punishment." What a contradiction of God's
holiness! I have heard this tune of "grace" played so
loudly that any thought that sin might have consequences
was drowned—and I have watched those who believed
such a song drown in their first experience of God's chas-
tening. To say that God would not deal with sin is a denial of God's very existence. This is the same thought that
the wicked man had in the Psalm—"All his thoughts are,
'There is no God' " (Psalms 10:4). This does not mean that
this wicked person thinks these words over and over; it
tells us that all of the wicked's thoughts are God-denying.
No, I cannot imagine any of these believers actually thinking *those* words either—maybe something more like,
"There is no God of judgment."

What a former pastor of mine called "the Chocolate
Pudding God" is very fashionable—a God so soft and

sweet that He would never become angry or lift His hand in punishment. This modern theology divides God up into New and Old Testament versions as if it had been *God* who had been changed (and was in need of changing) by the power of the Cross instead of rebellious humanity. But God is the same yesterday, today, and forever (see Hebrews 13:8). Yes, the *covenant* has changed. God, on the other hand, has *not*.

We need to be more like Him; He should not be in our chocolate pudding image. Grace and mercy are not opposites of justice but components of justice. Otherwise, God would have to be unjust to show mercy. God has created the entire universe with laws that reflect His character. Sowing and reaping is one of those immutable laws. Sin *always* costs; it cost God His dear Son. Jesus is a lawful avenue of grace and mercy within the just structure of God's universal law. Christ's blood pays the price of justice in the heavenly courts of eternity, but God, as our Father, still chastens His children for disobedience. If He did not, we would not be His children (see Hebrews 12:8).

A variation on the no-consequences theme is the peculiar belief that forgiveness of sins means that the consequences of sin are supposed to vanish. The drunkard who finally repents of his years of drunkenness and abuse of his family is often surprised when his wife still wants a divorce. The repentant thief is amazed when the police come to his door over a crime committed long ago, before his conversion, and they still want to prosecute.

Most of this stems from failure to acknowledge that sin has two effects:

1. It separates one from God—a condition remedied by our repentance and subsequent washing in the blood of Christ.

2. It unleashes evil into the world—evil which follows the law of sowing and reaping.[9]

The prime example is the story of David's repentance for his sin with Bathsheba. Note that the prophet Nathan gives David a list of the future consequences of his great evil and immediately follows by saying, "The Lord has taken away your sin."[10]

God did take some of the penalty away from David when He forgave him—after all, David was not executed as his crimes called for. But David was a long way from being clear of the backwash of his evil deeds.

Whatsoever a man sows, he *still* will also reap; Old or New Testament. God is not mocked.

"You shall surely not die," the temptation comes.

"Oh, yes, you will," comes the response of eternity.

Another Helping of Chocolate Pudding

The man had been crippled since birth. He barely made his way along the streets as the wasting disease had shriveled his legs. He had become a follower of The Way over a year ago and had harbored hopes that he would be healed of his malady, but that had not happened.

Now he hobbled on his crutch toward the little Roman hovel where Paul—formerly Saul of Tarsus—lived chained to a Praetorian guard. *Perhaps this time*, thought the man hopefully as he parted the coarse curtain that covered the entrance to Paul's dim dwelling.

"Ah, Marcus," called Paul as the man entered. "At last we can speak. Sit down! Sit down!" Paul indicated a large cushion. After they had settled and exchanged a greeting kiss and some words, Paul launched into the purpose for which he had summoned Marcus.

"I've noticed, Marcus, that you are having some difficulty in your walk with the Lord." Paul paused and Marcus acknowledged the statement with a nod and downcast eyes. "Well, I discern that your problem comes from your being angry with God." Marcus looked up and opened his mouth. Paul raised his hand to still any response. "Don't go into denial about it, Marcus. It is well known that you have been praying for a healing and that you have become bitter about not having received it. Now, I don't know when or if you will be healed, but I know you are hurting over it. My counsel to you is that you need to vent that anger before it causes further problems—you need to tell God you are angry with Him for not healing you. Go ahead and yell at Him and let it all out. God will understand—He knows your hurts and your anger. . . ."

Cut! Wait a minute! What's going on here? Paul would never say such a thing!

In the mouth of Paul the apostle such counsel sounds out of place, ridiculous, yet, acknowledged leaders in the church today give just such advice. And they do so regularly on radio and television. God has become a big punch-pillow for "Christian" transactional analysis. But if those kind of words are ludicrous in the mouth of Paul the apostle (or *any* Bible writer), why do we passively allow such drivel being spouted by our preachers? Did I say, "allow"? How about "swallow whole"?

I have heard God described as the ultimate psychologist as though He passively listens to our problems in true Rogerian, nondirective, and above all, *nonjudgmental* style. Jesus, they tell us, will allow us to "self-actualize" and self-realize our solutions. And why not? This is precisely the tack that most Christian psychologists take—the Carl Rogers nondirective approach. Why shouldn't believers see God this way when all of the "Biblical" counselors use this method?

The picture one gets is that God's *primary* goal in the universe is to promote individual "personal growth" of believers. The fact that much of the "growth" is so personal that no one else can see it seems to be inconsequential. For all this alleged growth of individuals, there is no corresponding progress in personal holiness. To the contrary, Christians caught up in the pulse-taking, introspective world of sanctified therapies are so self-absorbed that even God has a hard time finding a spot to land in their lives.

Here we find God transformed, changed into the likeness of corruptible man and of birds and four-footed animals and crawling creatures and psychologists (see Romans 1:22–23), *nonjudgmental* psychologists, that is.

"Scream at God," they advise, while Scripture says, "Woe to the one who quarrels with his Maker. . . . Will the clay say to the potter, 'What are you doing?' "[11]

"God won't mind (You shall surely not die)," they further urge foolishness. Meanwhile, Scripture warns, "And all who were angry at Him shall be put to shame."[12]

"But God is *Love*," they whine. "Perfect love casts out all fear, so we shouldn't fear God." "The fear of the LORD," *God* says, "is the beginning of wisdom."[13]

The whole degeneration of the church's awe for God began with the idea that God no longer judged sin, but these only mistook God's long-suffering for permissiveness (see 2 Peter 3:8–13). Seeing this frustrates believers who ache for God's righteousness, but they cling to the psalm's admonition, "Fret not yourself because of evildoers, be not envious toward wrongdoers. For they will wither quickly like the grass, and fade like the green herb."[14]

Here again, the believer is tempted to discount the judgment of God because the wicked "prospers in his way," but God plainly declares that His justice will prevail against the wicked, whether that is you or someone else. The question is, "When the evidence of your eyes convinces you that sin goes unpunished, will you believe the Word of God or the finite sight of your eyes? Will that sight convince you to sin, or will you fear God?"

We have all seen and heard of many who have vented anger against God and those who have treated Him as a tool for personal growth. Yet we see no fire from heaven, we see none stricken with sudden illness, no catastrophic judgments. Is this proof that the Serpent was right saying, "You shall surely not die if you yell at God"?

Yet, God's people are so afraid to be unfashionable that they cannot discern that massive national droughts, AIDS, growing ranks of predatory rapists and serial killers, and corrupted public officials are all, in fact, judgments from God. If we cannot even see these obvious divine retributions, how would we even know what things constituted judgments on the church? And even if there are no current judgments, does that mean there will be none? Many seem to think so.

Church discipline is now considered "unloving." And when "Christian" psychobabblers denounce Scripture's commands to remove unrepentant, sinning brethren, they offer the excuse that confrontation and disfellowship would damage the sinner's self-esteem and make "growth" impossible. They tout a "better, more compassionate way" than God's holy command to deal with the sinner's "problems." And despite the fact that an unrepentant sinner's destination is hell, the church does not blanch at this open rejection of God's Word.

Robert Schuller, the "possibility thinking" preacher of the infamous Crystal Cathedral, warns against preaching on "social ethics" (i.e., sin and righteousness) during Sunday sermons for fear that it might turn some away. He suggests that the place for "ethical discussions" (as if right and wrong were open for discussion) is "in the classroom where there can be dialogue." Schuller also "cautioned against sermons laden with scriptural [sic] references."[15] Well, let's toss out Peter's Pentecost message, Stephen's damning diatribe before the Sanhedrin, and all of Jesus' teachings—too many Bible verses and "social ethics." The effects of Jonathan Edward's sermon, "Sinners in the Hands of an Angry God," must have been a fluke.

But to the psychological types, "hurting people" seem to have unlimited time to "grow out of" their sin and heal up "their inner hurts" that *cause* them to sin. God, in this mentality, is gingerly and gently awaiting their "growth," not demanding their obedience. Of course, God would *never* confront them with their sin because He would know that they do not sin on purpose but due to unresolved "hurts." In this chocolate pudding bog, God hasn't the stomach or strength of character for judgment and condemnation. In other words, His Word is all bluff and bluster; He is too *merciful* to carry it through.

Some have gone so far as to teach that even Satan will be redeemed. Others say that after a short time of punishment, everyone will be saved. But all of these have the same ring—"You shall surely not die!"

Review

The third lie, "You shall surely not die," is rendered as:

- There is no death.
- There is reincarnation.
- There is no afterlife.
- There is an afterlife, but there is no hell.
- There are no consequences for sin.
- God will not see your sin.
- God is too merciful to punish for sin.

SOLD
BY SUGGESTION

J ust look at this," he said as he opened the velvet-covered box to reveal the watch. "Now, I've gotta get to L.A. so I'm willing to let this go for fifty dollars."

The timepiece glittered against the dark blue background. There was a pale blue plastic jewelry store price tag still wrapped around the golden watchband. The tiny writing appeared to say $350.

The salesman looked around the parking lot surreptitiously. A small urgency seemed to seep into his manner. The customer sensed the tension and looked over the watch in haste, pulled out $40 from his billfold.

"All I've got is forty," he said.

"You got a deal, man. Here's the watch."

The salesman moved quickly through the lot. Weaving between cars, the man was soon out of sight. The customer stuffed the watch under his car seat for later inspection as though he feared discovery and drove away from the shopping center.

❧ ❧ ❧

Many of you have had an experience with such a salesman and perhaps even bought from him. But, as those who have bought from him know, this man sold only suggestions. While his manner *suggested* that the item might be stolen, a careful check would reveal that the salesman was a licensed peddler. The dollar sign on the tag was actually a number sign, but your furtive look at the merchandise failed to catch the distinction. The name on the face implied that it was a Seiko, but it was merely a Seiku. The shine and glitter that evoked the belief that it was of fine craftsmanship dimmed on closer inspection. It looked more like it was manufactured by hammer, tongs, and chisel in Mexico—and it probably was.

But you were sold—sold on the suggestion.

"Now the serpent was more crafty than any beast of the field which the LORD God had made."[1] God's assessment of the Serpent is not overstated. Not all lies are actually told, many are simply suggested. In the first chapters, we looked at the indirect lies of Satan where he used questions rather than statements. Here we see the Snake has gotten bolder—his suggestion comes as a statement of fact, "For God doth know that in the day that you eat thereof . . ." or "God knows something important that He is not sharing with you."

Obviously, the temptation implies, God has some hidden motive and a hidden *something* that you should have. Perhaps God is seen as somewhat whimsical, playing a game of cosmic hide-and-seek. Maybe He has dark designs on your life or He may, like a wise mentor, have elected to let His creatures seek hidden knowledge from His carefully constructed clues.

Fatal Intentions

The ancient gods were most often malevolent. When they were not, they were merely unpredictable. No standard of good or evil guided their behavior, so mere humans were never sure of the deities' intentions. Even when they did "good" toward some person, it was often a very questionable good, such as being turned into eternal pillars in an Olympian temple. There was always something twisted about the gods, even when they were nice.

The temptation is often to view the God of the Bible with similar eyes—He *says* He's going to do us good, but you never know what He is going to do next. Even when we think we know what He will do, it is often distorted by this devious image of God. I have often heard Christians warn, "Don't pray for patience! The Bible says, 'Tribulation works patience,' so God will answer your prayer by sending you tribulation."

This popular advice is a wicked portrayal of God. While it is true that tribulation works patience, the verse does not say that tribulation is the only avenue to acquiring it. Such a statement makes God out to be a trickster, just lurking around until you pray for something that will cause problems in your life. It is a horrible misrepresentation of God to both believers and unbelievers.

Another familiar deception is believing that God cannot or will not save. Far from being a manifestation of low self-esteem, this belief asserts that a person—contrary to the plain statement of God's Word—is somehow unique in the entire creation. Satan must first convince this person that God does not love them, that is, that God is both a liar and a withholder of some good thing. The demonic deception that God does not love them is covered with the Biblical truth that all are unworthy, rebellious sinners. The modern remedy to this is to tell another kind of lie—the lie that man *is* worthy of God's love and Christ's incredible sacrifice. I will address the lie of self-esteem in chapter 7.

On the extreme end of this temptation are people who have believed that God is stringing them along like Judas Iscariot and will fry them in the end. Often new believers come under this delusion. They simply find it impossible to believe what God says about His own goodness—a patent refusal to believe God's Word.

The question really comes down to whether God has secrets. The answer is, "Of course He does!" But if one wants to know if God is keeping *needed* information from us, He is not. Nor is God attempting to obscure His will and His way from honest seekers. He has even been found by people like myself who were not even seeking Him (see Isaiah 65:1). While there is ample evidence in Scripture that God makes His Word dimmer and dimmer to those who reject Him, He leaves no man with the excuse, "I didn't know." God may make the way of the wicked hard, but all who seek Him will find Him, without exceptions.[2]

The Secret Knowledge

"The secret things belong to the LORD our God, but the things revealed belong to us and to our sons forever, that we may observe all the words of this law" (Deuteronomy 29:29). Yes, God has secrets. He keeps people on a "need to know" status. But what He keeps from us is not necessary for us to know. Yet occultists still seek the hidden mysteries and powers of the universe through meditations, drugs, enchantments, or contacts with familiar spirits. They try to pry the secrets of God out by force. Delusion is what they get for their trouble. Look at the pathetic results of the attempts of the late 1960s fascination with obtaining esoteric knowledge by using mind-altering drugs such as marijuana, L.S.D., and peyote. Some of the experimenters may be found in mental institutions and haunting the skidrows of our major cities, others are simply dead.

But Christians sometimes fare no better. The carnal drive for the forbidden still dwells within them. Some believers think it is profitable to seek out "the deep things of God" through esoterica such as numerology, typology, and symbology. Yearly attempts are made by some to divine the time of our Lord's return despite His admonition that "no man knows" this, not even the Son of Man. Mockery was heaped upon God and the church some time ago after the release of a booklet (a best-seller in Christian bookstores) called, "88 Reasons Why the Rapture Could be in 1988."[3] But it wasn't enough for the author to simply hide when he came up wrong, nor did he just admit that the whole thing was a mistake. The following year he published a new edition explaining why he had been one year off in his calculations.[4] I think that the author should have taken *two* years off in his writing career.

Naturally, the question of God's integrity may also be used inside-out. For instance, I have heard believers argue against the Biblical truth of a six-day creation. They will claim that the light of the stars should have taken millions of years to arrive at the earth. So, either God created the universe millions of years ago and let nature take its course or He created the universe with the light between the stars and earth in place. This last, they assert, would amount to God leaving false clues about the age of the universe, thus, they argue God's integrity would not allow Him to do that. In other words, either God *said* He created the cosmos recently but it is really old or He really made it recently and left evidence that suggests otherwise. God knows something important that He isn't sharing, the thought suggests.

In reality, God told us that in six days He created "the heavens and the earth, the sea and *all that is in them*" (Exodus 20:11, emphasis added). No Gap theories, no theistic evolution, no pre-Adamic creations, and certainly, according to Biblical chronology, *no* millions and millions of years. The simple answer to the starlight question is right in God's Word (where else?).

God's plainly stated reasons for creating the stars had nothing to do with determining the age of the cosmos. God says, "He made the stars also. And God placed them in the expanse of the heavens *to give light on the earth, and to govern the day and the night, and to separate the light from the darkness*" (Genesis 1:16–18, emphasis added). In verse 14 we are told that all of the heavenly luminaries are "for signs, and for seasons, and for days and years."

God did not simply forget to mention that the stars were for calculating the age of creation; He simply did not make them for that purpose. The argument about light-speed would not be such an effective lie if we spent more time studying God's purpose in creating things instead of operating on our faulty assumptions. But it is clearly part of carnal human nature to surmise that God has hidden that knowledge from us in spite of His clear revelation of the truth. This mistrust is especially appalling coming from those who seem ever so anxious to claim every promise in the Book. But when you claim the promises, you must believe the text. You cannot logically claim the promises based on the integrity of God one moment and question the veracity of His creation account the next.

Underlying both Christian and non-Christian efforts to unlock secret knowledge lurks the assumption that God is either withholding what is good and hoarding it for Himself, or He has intended for people to launch out from His revealed truth and blaze new trails into unrevealed realms. While this idea may have a certain luster, it is a fundamental denial of God's good intent and would cast us adrift in a universe of possible beliefs without any objective way to check our facts. How would we know, for instance, that channeling was not simply a "more mature" form of revelation once we have left God's Word behind as if it were a child's fancy? Perhaps polygamy is "a step above" monogamy. Who would know? Who could say for certain?

Bootstrap Theology

I remember that the fairy tales of my youth often presented a young man who "set out to make his fortune" or went off "to see the world." These were presented as normal and healthy actions for youth. After having been raised and taught by their fathers, young men were expected to go out and expand their horizons beyond the scope of their homes. After trials and tribulations the wandering son is successful in finding his "fortune," usually in the form of a princess-bride and vast riches. The theme is recurrent in literature and entertainment.

The Biblical presentation on this subject, however, is markedly different. Luke 15:11–32 records a similar story with a different result. The son in this parable left the God-given security of his home for the unknown and the end was disaster. He found his "fortune" in corn husks and hog slop. The wandering son returns repentant at the end—but he had to give up the pig swill first.

For man to bootstrap himself above the revealed Word of God and explore new realms of ethics and spirituality may sound ideal, but the "new ethical territory" is a spiritual hog trough.

For many, including believers, the so-called sciences are the route to this uncharted (actually, *forbidden* is the better word) land. Alleged scientific proof is taken as gospel even when it patently denies Biblical teaching. Theologians and theorizers will contort the Scriptures beyond recognition to fit the current archaeological dig. Yet, as usually happens, when evidence emerges a few years later to confirm the Biblical text, these same people shed their former distorted theory like snake skin and wriggle into Bible literalism. Suddenly, now that it is "scientific," they can believe the Word.

Amazingly, nonbelieving scientists are sometimes more willing to recognize the irony than believers, who *should* have the edge. Atheist astronomer, Robert Jastrow says:

> For the scientist who has lived by his faith in the power of reason, the story ends like a bad dream. He has scaled the mountains of ignorance; he is about to conquer the highest peak; as he pulls himself over the final rock, he is greeted by a band of theologians who have been sitting there for centuries.[5]

Others are less honest. When they discover, for instance, that all the real evidence points to instant creation of life on earth, they retreat into more bizarre theories of origins—theories such as the one that life was brought here by aliens. These last are members of the ABC (Anything But Christ) club. Their biases cancel their science because they, without proof, *exclude* certain conclusions from consideration.

But of all the modern "sciences," psychology heads the list of places where people seek the secrets God has not revealed in the Bible.[6] While believers insist on the doctrine of the fallen nature of man, the psychological presumption of the goodness of man takes precedence *in actual practice*. When pastors counsel, when believers advise, Maslow comes before Moses and Carl Rogers supersedes Christ Jesus.

As an example, one well-known radio minister explained that when she was young, preachers hammered away at warnings against the sin of pride. Even her preacher father railed regularly against pride, she indicated, and it was a major theme of visiting speakers as well. She went on to say, "But, now we know that it isn't pride but low self-esteem that is the problem."

You see? God didn't tell us everything (by her implication). Perhaps God was unaware of just how terrible a problem low self-esteem was when He penned the Scriptures. Could it be time for Him to revise?

But beneath all this is the unspoken assumption that God wants us to boldly go where no man has gone before and discover new moralities and new ethics. Here is the idea that the Word of God is merely a starting point for spirituality—an ethereal pabulum—to be used until we can digest the strong meat of human reason.

The Serpent's lie echoes through the millennia.

Review

The fourth lie, "For God doth know that in the day that you eat thereof . . ." is rendered as:

- God is keeping important knowledge from you.
- God is not concerned for what is good for you or mankind.
- God is hoping that you will "strike out on your own."

S I X

THE EGOISM
OF ENLIGHTENMENT

S o God has a secret and you want to know it? Fallen
human nature has a tremendous attraction toward
what it perceives as enlightenment, secret knowledge, or
"inner circles." This is a perversion of the natural, God-
given curiosity in man. So when the Serpent told Eve,
"God knows that if you eat it, *then your eyes will be
opened*," he was hooking into a very powerful drive—the
drive for knowledge. And already having removed Eve
from the foundation of God's Word, it was easier to tempt
her to acquire knowledge apart from Him. Satan even
seemed to imply that it may even be God's will that Eve
"mature" in this way by exercising her initiative to seek
enlightenment.

By succumbing to this temptation Eve set the stage for
the myriad false religions and mystery cults—with their
secret knowledge and their arcane means of enlightenment—and for the entire humanistic educational system
as well. For Eve to believe that the simple eating of a fruit
would grant special knowledge is akin to some of the

modern diet cults' claims that their regimen will enhance one's spiritual life. The implication that truth can come from some other source than those authorized by the living God casts man adrift in an endless universe of guesswork.

But the fallen human spirit seems to savor forbidden knowledge. As Proverbs 9:17 acknowledges, "Stolen water is sweet; and bread eaten in secret is pleasant." Even the seducer, the woman of folly, who quotes this proverb baits her snare with "knowledge."

Such groups as the Rosicrucian Order directly appeal to the "heritage [of the] mystery schools of ancient Egypt which developed and flourished circa 1400 B.C."[1] Early church gnostic heretics claimed such "hidden knowledge," and modern gnostics have trumped up spurious "gospels" which purport to present these hidden truths. They claim that the true meaning of Scripture is occluded by typology and numerology not understood by today's Bible reader and that introduction into special "mysteries" is needed.

At times this knowledge is proffered by discarnate spirits like Ramtha, an alleged thirty-five thousand-year-old warrior, whose personality is "channeled" through a spiritist or necromancer. One such spiritist, Chuck Little, claims to channel Yahweh, but his teaching does not sound at all like the Yahweh of the Bible.[2]

Often these forms of knowledge are entirely removed from the arena of the verifiable. Many occult practices like acupuncture, crystal-therapy, and touch therapy are based on undetectable emanations of certain people or substances on the ch'i (energy) traveling through meridians (psychic pathways) in the body.

Secular versions of the secret knowledge lie are evident in scientism—the deification of science. Beginning with the worship of Nebo, Babylon's god of knowledge and science, God-denying "sciences" have been used to convince people that the Truth is simply not scientific. The scientific method of investigation has been obscured so that only the "priests" of the profession are able to truly comprehend their methods. The rest of the people must take by faith the pronouncements of Carl Sagan and his ilk.

Even today, the bait dangles every time man faces a problem and someone says, "Education is the answer!"

But if knowledge, hidden or otherwise, is the answer, then God is apparently only interested in saving those who are capable of seeking out and understanding that knowledge. Of course, God must then *exclude* the mentally retarded and the uneducated, but that doesn't sound like the God I know!

In with the In-Crowd

In the last book of the C. S. Lewis space trilogy, *That Hideous Strength*, one of the central characters, Mark, sought to become part of the "inner-circle." When he finally was accepted into an academic post at Bracton College, he was sure he had made it, only to discover an inner circle within the academia of Bracton. It wasn't long, though, before he had penetrated the circle only to discover a hidden conclave inside that group.

Mark's efforts in the story take him through all the inner circles until he reaches the ultimate "in" group— several men whom Mark deeply respects. But in the end these men all are found doing naked obeisance and human sacrifice to a drooling, discorporate head which has been mechanically kept alive and houses a thoroughly demonic mind.

In the end, the three men stood naked before the Head—gaunt, big-boned Straik; Filostrato, a wobbling mountain of fat; Whither, an obscene senility. Then the high ridge of terror from which Filostrato was never again to descend, was reached; for what he thought impossible began to happen. No one had read the dials, adjusted the pressures, or turned up the air and the artificial saliva. Yet words came out of the dry gaping mouth of the dead man's head. "Adore!" it said.[3]

Mark, wounded, escapes the bloody scene and the story goes on to relate, "For he now thought that with all his life-long eagerness to reach an inner circle he had chosen the *wrong* circle."

The wrong circle indeed! Lewis's dark work serves as a parable of the hypnotic draw of an evil "circle." All too often it is the appearance of knowledge and the drive to be accepted by a select group of "betters" that drives us to act, rather than our desire to be accepted by our Better (God). In hopes of being able to mingle with the elite, we study the leading psychologists and philosophers. Our motive determines the outcome. If we see their words as springboards into the gospel of Christ, the way Paul the apostle did on Mars Hill, we maintain the central truth of God's Word and are enriched by the encounter. But when we secretly believe that these men had truths not found in the Bible, we are seduced away from God, and the words "your eyes shall be opened" echo in the spiritual ears.

Associate Professor William Kirk Kilpatrick of Boston College describes just such a descending spiral:

I began to lose interest in the Christian faith in graduate school. That was when I discovered psychology. I didn't realize I was losing interest in Christianity; *I merely thought I was adding something on.* But before long I had shifted my faith from one to the other.

There was no reason not to. As far as I could see, there was no essential difference between the two. I had been reading the most liberal theologians—that is to say, the most psychologized ones—and from what I could gather, the important thing in religion was not Bible or creed but simply loving other people. I thought I could swing that easily enough without the help of church or prayers. Such practices, I assumed, were intended for *those who hadn't attained awareness.* (emphases added)[4]

Kilpatrick says he slowly surrendered all of his faith to gain acceptance among those who had "attained awareness." He adds,

I felt no need to renounce cherished beliefs. They simply melted away like March snowmen. More often than not, the melting-away process was aided and abetted by theologians who were eager to remove difficult parts of the faith. . . . But like a child of immigrant parents, ashamed of their accent and anxious to assimilate, I had arrived at a stage of life where I would have been deeply embarrassed just to be associated with it.[5]

Kilpatrick's experience can be repeated countless times by believers who become involved in many of the so-called sciences that offer a kind of knowledge that appeals to pride. The same pride that tempted Satan to go beyond God and usurp His power, tempts men, often subtly, to go beyond God's Word in search of unholy knowledge.

Knowledge of the Unholy

Proverbs repeatedly admonishes us to seek knowledge as precious. But that same Bible also tells us that *all* the treasures of wisdom and knowledge are hidden in Christ Jesus. God's Word talks about mysteries and hidden knowledge, but in Christ, mysteries are revealed and what is hidden is hidden from those who will not submit to Christ. Outside of Christ are only snares.

Yet almost daily I hear of believers touting knowledge from the world as the answer for problems within the church. Some offer the occult practices of hypnosis and dream therapy as replacements for repentance; positive thinking for faith toward God; regression to birth trauma or flotation tanks for baptism; massage for the laying on of hands; and self-esteem for self-examination.

In the more mundane world, questionable fund-raising practices are adopted by churches from the textbooks of PR firms who have worked for political parties and doubtful charities. Madison Avenue, rather than the Bible, guides our outreach programs. We have added bowling alleys and swimming pools to our churches to "attract people to Christ," while abortion clinics just blocks away ply their grisly trade day after day on women who just need a place to stay or help with medical bills for them to save their babies.

A more crass use of knowledge of the unholy was the report of a Dallas, Texas, church that adopted modern marketing techniques to bring in congregants. "The old style church growth [I suspect this means preaching and teaching God's Word] no longer works," said Rev. Peter Paulson. This church—and many others since in the notorious "church growth movement"—conducted surveys, targeted well-paid, well-educated families, hired ministers in their thirties who demonstrated that they were "hungriest for success," and finally ran a successful ad campaign.

Paulson further explained, "You no longer can come into a community and put up a cinder-block building on a back street. God is an orderly God. And if you prepare yourself well, then God intervenes, which is the nature of a miracle."[6]

Along this same line, the leader of the early seventies "Christian" ad campaign called, "I Found It," a former Coca-

Cola advertising executive, said, "In New Testament times God used miracles to bring people, but we don't need miracles. We have radio and television and the other media."

"I Found It" was a multimillion dollar failure, but generally the Dallas, Texas, marketing approach has succeeded in reaching its goals. A Gallup poll from early 1984 indicated that there was a 11.7 percent increase in giving and surging attendance.[7]

The bad news came later that year when the same pollster delivered a ringing indictment against the sales approach to church growth.

> Gallup says in a summary: "Religion is growing in importance among Americans, but morality is losing ground. . . ."
>
> But while religious concern is up, he [Gallup] says, morality paradoxically is down and he cites the rising figures for crime, drug and alcohol abuse, business cheating and divorce.[8]

God said He has given the foolishness of preaching to save the lost (see 1 Corinthians 1:21). Evidently, the Rev. Paulson and the promoters of "I Found It" felt they had had their eyes opened to a better way through some secret extrabiblical knowledge. But despite the nickels-and-noses "success" of their methods, there was a deterioration of Truth.

Educational Malpractice

Let me warn you: From time to time someone will say, "You will know the truth, and the truth will make you free." But it is not true.

What? You think I'm wrong? You probably think that quote comes from John 8:32 and you are right. But I still say it is untrue—untrue unless the beginning of the quote in verse 31 is included.

What Jesus actually said is, "*If you abide in My word,* then you are truly disciples of Mine; and you shall know the truth." The implication is that your obedience to the Word that you already know qualifies you for both further revelation and freedom. But most people believe, or want to believe, that truth (knowledge, education, etc.) will, of itself, set someone free.

In the secular world, this belief may be a holdover from our vanishing Christian consensus and of this misunderstanding of Jesus' words. Generally, faith in knowledge is firmly anchored to an unbiblical belief in the natural goodness of man—what philosopher Richard Weaver described as "hysterical optimism." This pollyanna view is on display in the self-esteem, self-actualization tenets of psychology.

But a more popular manifestation is the recurrent mantra, "What we need is more education," which is chanted at the mention of nearly any societal problem. This is the very heart of "your eyes shall be opened" or "once you *know* enough, your problems will be solved."

Planned Parenthood and their band used this argument as their excuse to inject sex education into public schools in the early 1960s, ostensibly to curb the teen pregnancy rate. The immediate and subsequent rise in teen pregnancies has only given rise to louder chants of "We need *more* sex education!" Greater jumps in the numbers of teen mothers took place as they began to educate girls on using and acquiring the pill. Even Planned Parenthood's own studies show that "unintended pregnancies" increased among contraceptive users who had received sex-ed services.[9]

In the early 1970s, many states and localities decided to try to stop drug abuse with massive education campaigns in grade schools. I think anyone can see that the young people from that time are our most prominent drug users today.

Most of the promoters of these schemes are blind to their theory's failures, but others—now awakened—are perplexed. Actually, the answer is simple: Weeds are easy to grow, but one must *cultivate* desirable plants. Hothouse plants survive and produce *better* after being transplanted outdoors than plants raised outside from seed.

Long, drawn-out, explicit descriptions of sex or drug use actually lowers inhibitions about becoming involved. While this is especially true of young people, adults are not immune. There is a tacit approval in "openness"—and today the approval is much more than tacit. Most of the public education versions of Safe Sex have gone beyond "value-free" and positively glorify sexual activity.

Now back to the weeds: The rebellious nature of man will invariably use "value-free" knowledge to increase its wickedness. The carnal nature of man soaks up such education as fertilizer for its fruit of corruption.

So when believers are afraid that they will weaken their children, spiritually or naturally, by isolating them from evil in their youth, they should recall the truth about hothouse plants. Hothouse plants are *stronger and more productive.* Just as the weed-free, well-watered environment of the greenhouse produces a stronger plant, so home school, Christian school, church, and selected friendships will improve a child's chances of resisting the world's tug. I qualify that with the words "improve chances" because children are *not* plants. The illustration, however, has some validity.

Another arena for the education solution myth is the area of counseling. The assumption in counseling, whether Christian or secular, is that once the patient understands the source of his difficulty, he will be able to overcome it. Repeated studies and personal experience verify that relief comes when a person changes his behavior in the present, not when he discovers some past "scar" that has "caused" the problem. Studies show that it is the person who truly wants to change that is most helped and that nearly any treatment will be effective. Yet, the counseling world continues to market the idea that the mere knowledge of the "cause" will bring relief. But such a belief denies the culpability of the individual for his own condition. When people learn to transfer guilt because of this method, it effectively removes them from the reach of Christ because 1 John 1:9 tells us that the blood of Christ cleanses us when we *acknowledge* our sin. As a friend once told me, "The blood of Jesus cleanses from sin, not excuses or reasons."

None of this is to imply that knowledge or education are evil. Even Jesus' statement about the truth making one free shows that knowledge is effective, if accompanied by a holy desire to do right. This is where the book of Proverbs commends knowledge. Knowledge with the wisdom to use it correctly is of great value, but information fed to an evil mind will be distorted into wickedness.

When the temptation, "your eyes shall be opened," comes, make sure that what your eyes will see is what God is showing.

Review

The fifth lie, "your eyes shall be opened," can be rendered as:

- You will share in exclusive mystery knowledge.
- You will attain true enlightenment.
- Education is the answer.

SEVEN

GARDEN GODS

"Thou art God." "You create your own reality." "Name it and claim it." "Everything is God." "God is nothing."

These statements may seem disparate, but in reality they follow the same line—"You shall be as gods."

The promise of the "inner circle" exclusiveness—*godhood*—was the glitter of Satan's Garden lure. The prospect snagged Eve's attention. Possibly she imagined that God *wanted* her to be as a god. She could almost sense the personal power she would experience as a goddess—speak, and things would be created; think, and they would appear. Imagine the *good* she could do. Perhaps she felt this would please God.

But this temptation makes man, individually or collectively, the center of all things. God's Word becomes secondary or even outdated. A new standard is established. Man's needs, man's wants, man's desires becomes the central question, and *man* becomes the answer. *Man* makes the final decisions. This, at its center, is humanism.

However, the West is today also undergoing a resurgence in the ancient nature worship religions which preach pantheism—that *everything* is god. Whether they perceive the whole as one goddess, as with Gaia worship, or that everything has individual spirits, as the animists claim, the result is the same. In Romans 1, God rails against those who "worship and serve the creature rather than the Creator" (v. 25).

Robert J. L. Burrows from the Spiritual Counterfeits Project in Berkley, California, reminds us, "Dostoevsky said anything is permissible if there is no God. But anything is also permissible if everything is God. There is no way of making any distinction between good and evil."[1] The elimination of a separate (holy) God also destroys objective principles of good and evil, a topic we shall discuss in greater detail in the next chapter.

Of course, the Serpent knew that no one could truly displace God. He had already tried to usurp God's throne and failed. But the *same lure* that had dragged him down from the heights of heaven to the craggy abyss of hell amply supplies him with human company in his eternal misery. There are three ways for him to make God impotent in the life of man—one is to ignore Him (difficult), another is to elevate man or mankind or nature to the status of God (much easier and very appealing to man's pride), and the last is to lower God to being like man (leaving man with a God he didn't have to strive after). This last is a favorite of modern theologians who continually strive to humanize Jesus—to hold Him as a mere example rather than a savior. This was the same diabolical motive that spawned the movie *The Last Temptation of Christ* which portrayed Jesus as an ordinary man tossed by the same lusts, passions, and confusions as the rest of humanity.

The lie of human divinity can be framed in a more subtle way than overt, bogus claims of godhood. It is easily couched in terms of ESP or telekinesis, mind over matter—innate personal power. Techniques such as visualization and creative thought are offshoots of this version of the god-man myth. Visualization teachers assert that we "create" our own life and circumstances—a total denial of the sovereignty of God. Shirley MacLaine asserts, "We understand we all have our own truth because we all create our own reality. . . . Nature follows the mind. You begin to see you literally are the creator of everything—including the weather."[2]

Still, one of the most powerful secular versions of the godhood lie is found in psychology. With its self-esteem teachings and self-actualization, it clearly denies the fallen nature of man and his natural propensity for evil while teaching that man is naturally drawn to what is right "for him" much like a self-correcting guided missile. This is the presumption of Carl Rogers' nondirective counseling methods. If man is good at the core, all he needs to do is to learn to "listen to the inner voice" and he will make the right choices. Rogers claimed that the counselor was merely to provide an atmosphere of acceptance in which this inner voice could best be heard. Rogerian style is the most widely emulated method in modern counseling chambers, even among believers. All this is merely secular paganism which has exchanged "godhood" for "goodhood." This denial of God's holiness and man's sinfulness makes the act of Jesus Christ on the cross utterly meaningless. If man is basically good, he does not need a savior.

There Is No God

Joshua sat quietly in the dark of the back seat. He was normally a quiet boy, and usually was softly sleeping on these long, nighttime rides back to town after Bible study.

This time he was awake and his five-year-old brain was working overtime chewing on deep thoughts.

"Dad?" he said.

"Yes, Joshua?" I answered.

A moment passed while Joshua collected his words. "Dad, I think that when people don't believe in God, it's because they think that *they* are God."

⁂ ⁂ ⁂

Quite a point for a little boy, but very revealing. While it may seem contradictory to say "You shall be as gods" and "There is no God," the two are ultimately compatible. The final denial of God's existence could only come from those who felt that they themselves were the ultimate authority. After all, the proclaiming of a universal negative (There is no God) is tantamount to a claim to all knowledge. In order to say for certain that there is no God, one must lay claim to having searched the entire universe with every possible means of detection.

In this way, the so-called atheist takes on the attributes of God while he claims there is no such being. The atheist becomes the authority on good and evil, or existence and nonexistence. He alone decides that the supernatural is not real and then has the foolish pride to claim that his beliefs are scientific.

G. K. Chesterton answers such a claim:

My belief that miracles have happened in human history is not a mystical belief at all; I believe in them upon human evidences as I do in the discovery of America. Somehow or other an extraordinary idea has arisen, [that] disbelievers in miracles consider them coldly and fairly, while believers in miracles accept them only in connection with some dogma. The fact is quite the other way. The believers in miracles accept them (rightly or wrongly), only because they have some evidence for them. The disbelievers deny them (rightly or wrongly) because they have a doctrine against them.[3]

The same may be said for the existence of God. A good example is the current scientific debate on creation and evolution. Many scientists, who are supposed to let the facts lead them, are so mortified when evidence seems to support instantaneous creation that they take headlong plunges into lunatic theories or hypotheses with absolutely *no* supporting evidence. This is because they begin with the presupposition that God does not exist and that He did not create the universe. The fact that these presuppositions render all their work unscientific does not seem to occur to them.

Such a presupposition was in evidence in the 1967 Nobel Peace Prize winner, Dr. George Wald, when he said,

> When it comes to the origin of life on this earth, there are only two possibilities: creation or spontaneous generation (evolution). There is no third way. Spontaneous generation was disproved 100 years ago, but that leads us only to one other conclusion: that of supernatural creation. We cannot accept that on philosophical grounds (personal reasons); therefore, we choose to believe the impossible: that life arose spontaneously by chance.[4]

These "scientists" utterly refuse to live in a universe with God, so they, defying all truth, create one without Him. As I have said before, the man who says there is no God worships the god he sees in his mirror.

If *You* Are God, Who Am I?

An Oriental wise man once awoke from a dream. He had dreamt he was a butterfly. But as he told another about the dream he became confused.

"Am I a man who has dreamed he was a butterfly," he asked himself, "Or am I a butterfly still dreaming that I am a man?"

This well-known tale is supposed to be a demonstration of some sort of wisdom or profundity. To me, it illustrates a childish, untrained thought process and foolishness. It is, however, an adequate picture of the confusion inherent in the free-wheeling, unsettled "reality" of temporized truth.

The "Thou art God" teachings of the neopagans present just this same dilemma: If I am God, are you just a creation of my mind? Or is it the other way around? If we are all God, why do we disagree on so much and how did we all end up with the same "reality"? Was Josef Stalin God? Charles Manson (*he* thought he was)?   Adolf Hitler? Once we find out who exactly *is* God, how are we to respond to him? The questions are endless. And they become even more bizarre when we believe two of the variants on this theme: "God is everything and everything is God" and "Mankind (collectively) is God." One is pantheism while the other posits a gestalt of sentient beings.

Singular godhood is quite openly taught by the neo-Hindus but more covertly within the church via "power" theology. Mormons, who are not Christian, teach, like the Hindus, that man is an evolving god, but that man can only attain this status through Mormon baptism. But Christian groups are adopting some similar heresies. These are usually linked to one of the "power" sects, the name-it-and-claim-it bunch. Most often they tenaciously latch onto a couple of passages to prove their assertions:

1. The place where Jesus says to the Jews, "Has it not been written in your Law, 'I said, you are gods'?"[5]

2. The ever popular, "The kingdom of God is within you."[6]

I will briefly address each of these after I point out that Christians should be alarmed when they find their ministries trying to prove the same doctrines as the New Age pagans, especially when using the same isolated verses of Scripture. The same neopagans who utterly reject the Bible use verses like these to prove their deceptions just as the Serpent used a twisted word from God to bolster his argument with Eve.

Jesus' quote from Psalms 82:6 was first made to his opponents among the Jews. Was He trying to open their eyes to the fact that they were gods? Hardly! The scathing sarcasm of Jesus' words fairly leaps off the page. "Why do you say that I blaspheme when I say I am the Son of God? Doesn't your own Law tell you that *you* are gods?" Jesus cut to the quick. These hypocrites obviously suffered from delusions of godhood, but they also knew the psalm. In the psalm the tone of God is derision, "I said, 'You are gods. . . . Nevertheless *you will die like men*" (Psalms 82:6–7, emphasis added). What a put-down! And Jesus just threw it back in their faces of pride. This verse proves nothing except that there are still men who think they are gods.

As for the second verse, I find it amazing that the very people who complain about the archaic language of the King James Bible will quote this version alone when saying, "The kingdom of God is within you." The modern translations more accurately render it "in your midst" rather than "within you." The word *within* here is perfectly consistent with Elizabethan English usage for "in your midst." It does not mean "inside you" as if the kingdom of Heaven resided inside the Pharisees. The context of the discussion indicates that Jesus was alluding to His divine presence as the kingdom. He told them not to be looking for signs of the approach of the kingdom because the kingdom was wherever the King was—namely, right in their midst. The kingdom is where the King is.

But it is not surprising that this temptation would be leveled against God's people since it was also aimed at His Son. In a harsh and stony desert after much fasting and prayer, Jesus was tempted with the words, "If You are the Son of God . . ." It has the familiar ring of today's prosperity teachers saying, "If you are one of the King's kids, God does not want you to be . . ." (Check one of the following.)

❐ Poor

❐ Sick

❐ Unhappy

❐ Any of the above

However, when most people claim godhood, they do so indirectly. They usually begin by attributing God's character and abilities to themselves—such as, the ability to decide finally on right and wrong. But the exaltation of *all* humanity to godhood seems to be more profane in that the attributes of God disappear altogether. Since each "part" of God has his or her own ideas about right and wrong (and none can gainsay "God"), the standard vanishes and becomes a matter of each god's preference. But today, the deification of mankind as a whole is best seen as a secular rather than religious manifestation. Most nonbelievers see man as the most advanced being in an evolving universe. By the law of survival-of-the-fittest, therefore, man is the pinnacle of all things. This gives him the right to decide on such things as right and wrong (when such concepts are needed) or life and death—decisions that were formerly viewed as God's territory.

These are all included under the humanism umbrella. Individually practiced, humanism determines what is right and wrong purely by its effect on the individual himself. Corporately seen, humanism's differentiation between good and evil rests solely on what is presently perceived as "good for humanity." This belief is obvious in the infamous *Humanist Manifestos I* and *II*. A couple of quotes from the two documents will suffice to illustrate.

> There is great danger in a final, and we believe fatal, identification of the word *religion* with doctrines and methods which have lost their significance and which are powerless to solve the problem of human living in the twentieth century. . . . Religious humanism maintains that *all associations and institutions exist for the fulfillment of human life.* (emphasis added)[7]
>
> We affirm that moral values derive their source from human experience. Ethics is autonomous and situational, needing no theological or ideological sanction.[8]

Could anyone claim more godlike prerogatives than these manifestos?

To the humanist, though, this all sounds completely logical. Bertrand Russell, though a notable humanist himself, commented, "If good and bad are decided by the results, how do we know if the results are good or bad?"

A telling comment, indeed. And God goes one better: "There is a way which seems right to a man, but its end is the way of death."[9]

Revival of Nature Worship

"The Goddess is alive and magic is afoot," the bumper sticker read. Another testified, "My other car is a broom."

Both were tokens of the revival of nature worship—the worship of Gaia, the goddess of nature.

Early pagans believed in nature gods—gods who were spirits of natural creatures such as the sun, stars, trees, or rain. They were less likely to believe that they themselves were divine. There was, to them, an essential "otherness" about divine beings. In the end, Satan had fooled them into believing in gods who were reduced to human proportions. Pantheism differs in that the godhead includes humans. But goddess worship views humans and all nature as *offspring* of a female god who is over all—a female replacement for the God of the Bible.

The environmental movement is steeped in this religious dogma. Even those who do not personalize nature as an independently sentient being present nature as a model of what is good and evil. They feel that nature will never steer us wrong. The ultimate defense for anything is its degree of naturalness. Of course, it was precisely this kind of thinking that supplied justification for the Nazis to "naturally" cull out the weaker, less-evolved strains of human beings. After all, this is precisely what happens in nature. Man is in the driver's seat; *he* interprets nature's signals of good and evil.

Believers, perhaps, do not realize that modern theology has been saturated with survival-of-the-fittest ideology. The chief of these is the simple acceptance of evolution as a true scenario of creation. What kind of character must a God have if He used millions of years of suffering, death, competition, and savagery to bring about the creation, and then say it is "good"? In a *fallen* world's natural order, the strong *do* survive, but Scripture enjoins us to seek out and protect the weak. God's Word also portrays a world, both in Eden and after His return, that will not be characterized by today's dog-eat-dog principle.

Even nature isn't natural. Man's fall profoundly corrupted the order of the rest of creation. Remember that the
creation was to be tended by man—not in some servile
way but as a benevolent master. Man's fall left a leadership vacuum that has since been replaced by chaos.

The Force—Sorcery

"I am the Power!" proclaimed He-man, the supernaturally
empowered cartoon character when he wished to be transformed from an ordinary person to his godlike alter-ego
identity. The incantation produced lightning flashes, bulg-
ing biceps, and supernatural abilities.

This child's cartoon show displays a mysterious power
available to man after repeating an enchanted mantra.
This portrays the ancient idea that there is universal
power for the taking if one knows the secret formula. The
more mystical nature worshipers believe that auras and
vibrations of power emanate from all of the cosmos. It is
just a matter, they say, of tapping into what the ancients
called "mana." Today, this same power is most often
called "the force" or "the god within."

With this power people are purportedly able to "create
their own reality" through visualization, dreams, mental
disciplines, enchantments, and the like. In recent years,
Christians have become involved in this ethereal power-
brokering through visualization, "prophecy" (name-it-
and-claim-it), positive thinking, and "prayers." The differences between them are negligible. In fact, I have heard
ministers admit that these techniques have been known
from ancient times and claim that they are available to
anyone—believer or unbeliever. There is no sense, they
say, in God's people being the only ones left out.

But let's look at this more closely. Compare what God's Word says with the words of the modern power purveyors.

Paganism	Bible
Thou art God.	I am the LORD, and there is no other; besides Me there is no God.[10]
	God is not a man, that He should lie.[11]
The power is within you.	Blessing and glory and wisdom and thanksgiving and honor and *power and might*, be to our God forever and ever. Amen.[12]
	All power is given unto me in heaven and in earth.[13]
Speak your desires into existence.	Every good thing bestowed and every perfect gift is from above, coming down from the Father of lights.[14]
You create your own reality.	For in six days *the LORD made* the heavens and the earth, the sea and *all* that is in them.[15]
	Where were you when I laid the foundation of the earth! . . . Have you ever in your life commanded the morning, and caused the dawn to know its place?[16]
	Which of you by taking thought can add one cubit unto his stature?[17]

This is only a small sampling of Scripture that refutes these common pagan teachings. Nearly any believer could make this same case with many more verses. But apparently that argument appears only in the "religious dogma" compartment of their minds because, in actual practice, many Christians use the techniques spawned by these pagan principles. Religious doctrine is one thing, they seem to say, the *real* world is another.

Yes, ancients have used these principles of paganism with various methods to manipulate reality for millennia, but that does not change the simple fact that it is sorcery. And no amount of christianizing or chanting "In Jesus' name" will reconcile these two distinct sets of beliefs. Teachings within the church that claim power for man or insist that God's power can be controlled by man are pure heresy—whether it is called positive (or possibility) thinking, visualization, or whatever, it presents a God who can be manipulated by the power of man's will.

God is sovereign. No man has been His counselor, much less His boss.

Steaming in Self

"To be born again means that we must be changed from a negative to a positive self-image."[18]

Somebody said this was the Me generation, and evidently the Me generation all feel they need more "Me." The most self-serving, self-indulgent crop of humans in modern history, it is said, suffers from not thinking highly enough of themselves. Religious figures inform them that when they think more highly of themselves (perhaps, than they ought), they will be born again in proper Biblical fashion.

The self-esteem teaching is not new. Its first appearance was framed as "You shall be as gods" but its name has always been pride. It is not surprising, then, that God-rejecting sciences promote pride. Psychology is chief among them. The theory is that if we value ourselves more, we will then value others more. In practice, people who focus on their own value become more and more self-absorbed and less likely to help others.[19]

However, many of the promoters of self-esteem are unwilling to associate the term with pride, but the more honest souls wade right in. Robert Schuller, the TV personality/preacher, is chief among those who spread this teaching within the church. Compare his words with the Bible.

> Schuller: "'Pride in being a human being is the single greatest need facing the human race today."[20]

> God: "God is opposed to the proud, but gives grace to the humble."[21]

> Schuller: "The cross sanctifies the ego trip."[22]

> God: "Pride goes before destruction, and a haughty spirit before stumbling."[23]

Believing psychologists equivocate, claiming to promote only self-confidence and self-respect. Yet, we rarely hear any warnings against pride from these Christian counselors. Scripture, on the other hand, is replete with such warnings and says *nothing whatsoever* about low self-esteem.

One well-known Christian author writes:

> The matter of personal worth is not only the concern of those who lack it. In a very real sense, the health of the entire society depends on the ease with which the individual members gain personal acceptance. *Thus, whenever the keys to self-esteem are seemingly out of reach for a large percentage of people, as in twentieth-century America, then widespread "mental illness," neuroticism, hatred, alcoholism, drug abuse, violence, and social disorder will certainly occur.* (emphasis his)[24]

Are all these problems from low self-esteem and not from the carnal nature's pride? It is difficult to imagine that God's Word would have *nothing* to say about something so utterly destructive in human lives. Perhaps God should have held off writing the Scriptures until He had had the chance to read Robert Schuller. One thing I can say with some degree of certainty is that the appearance of self-esteem teachings in the church has *preceded* the sharp rise in the divorce rate, suicide rate, drug and alcohol abuse rate, adultery and fornication rate, and teen pregnancy rate *inside the church*. The fact that the advent of this teaching was as recent as the early 1970s should not be lost here.

> Though it may seem surprising, the fact is that little more than a decade ago [1982] this topic was virtually unheard of in evangelical circles. A look at the copyright page of some of the more prominent volumes on the subject . . . reveals the significant fact that the earliest date among them is 1974.[25]

The fact that the Scriptures do not even obliquely address this issue and the fact that the doctrine has the briefest and most questionable of pedigrees should cause us great concern. But if self-esteem is, as it appears to be, a backhanded way of injecting old-fashioned pride into the church, we are indeed in much peril.

To paraphrase: Self-esteem goes before destruction.

Perhaps we will experience a great judgment from God for all of this self-worship. Robert Schuller says that we "need a theology that begins and ends with a recognition of every person's hunger for glory."[26] But Erwin W. Lutzer reminds us of an instructive Biblical example:

> King Nebuchadnezzar saw himself as Christian humanists recommend today: He had self-confidence, esteem, and apparently an integrated personality. He was a positive thinker whose great plans were realized.
>
> "Is this not Babylon the great, which I myself have built as a royal residence by the might of my power and

the glory of my majesty?" he asked (Daniel 4:30). His
hunger for glory was satisfied.

God's response was to smite him with insanity.[27]

Sometimes, when I look at the American church, I
wonder if we have not *already* been smitten.

Review

The sixth lie, "you shall be as gods," can be rendered as:

- You are God.
- Mankind is God.
- All nature is God.
- There is no God.
- You have secret, untapped powers.
- Nature has secret, untapped powers (mana).
- You create your own reality (health, wealth, etc.) in your mind.
- You are worthy of worship.

THE ABOLITION
OF GOOD AND EVIL

I t was a small party in an elegant flat overlooking the
city. Rupert, the professor of philosophy, was making
light of how many problems would be solved by legaliz-
ing murder—problems like long theater ticket lines. An
older gentleman was uncomfortable and offended by the
direction of the conversation and injected that Rupert
must be jesting.

Rupert indicated he was not. "Murder," he said, "is—
or should be—an art, and as such, the privilege of com-
mitting it should be reserved for those few who are really
superior individuals."

Brandon, a former student of Rupert's, chimed in
agreeably, "The few are those men of such intellectual and
moral superiority that they're above the traditional moral
concepts. Good and evil, right and wrong were invented
for the ordinary, average man—the inferior man—because
he needs them."

The older gentleman and his wife were astonished and
soon excused themselves from the *soirée*.

99

Later, a suspicious Rupert returned to the apartment only to find out that Brandon had strangled David, another of his former students, and had packed him in the wooden chest that had served as a refreshment buffet for the gathering.

Brandon, confident that Rupert, of all people, would understand, explained how he had strangled the unimportant life out of David as proof of his own superiority. He said the concepts had come straight from all his classes and conversations with the professor. But Rupert was having none of it.

"You've given my words a meaning that I never dreamed of," he said. "Tonight you've made me ashamed of every concept I've ever had of superior or inferior beings."

Then Rupert summoned the police.

ɕ ɕ ɕ

These were scenes from *Rope*, an Alfred Hitchcock movie, a work of fiction. In real life, it may have ended quite differently—with Professor Rupert congratulating Student Brandon for properly exercising his prerogative as a superior man, because in real life, this existential philosophy of "super men," first made popular in modern times by Nietzsche, has resulted in worldwide slaughter.

Nietzsche said, "He shall be the greatest who can be loneliest, the most concealed, the most deviant, the human being beyond good and evil, the master of his virtues, overrich in will."[1] The Nazi's believed it and acted. As Richard Weaver wrote, "Ideas have consequences."

Yet this horrid philosophy is merely another manifestation of the satanic invitation to "know good and evil." Others are:

- Good and evil are an illusion.
- There are no absolutes.
- You can't legislate morality.
- Something is good or evil depending on the situation.
- Religion is very personal; you must decide for yourself what is right between you and God.
- Good and evil are two sides of the same coin.
- No one can dictate what is right for *you*.
- Let us do evil that good may come.
- What is good in one culture may be evil in another.
- Different strokes for different folks.
- Do your own thing.

You have all heard these or ones very much like them. Today, we are inundated with attempts to distort, disguise, or redefine good and evil, but they are all rooted in the deception of Eve.

To suppose that Adam and Eve, even in innocence, did not know of the existence of good and evil is foolish. How would they otherwise have understood God's prohibition? They would not only have been lower than the angels, they would have had to be lower than the animals. Without this simple understanding, the prime pair could not have comprehended God's command not to eat of the tree of the knowledge of good and evil, much less understood the idea of reaping terrible consequences for disobedience.

"Knowing good and evil," as in the serpentine temptation, meant much more than knowing that the two existed. When the Serpent told Eve she would "know" good and evil, he used the word *yada'* which primarily means "to ascertain by seeing" or knowledge by personal experience, a *participation* in good and evil. Satan implies that to be like God she must *experience* both.

Chris Griscom, a New Age leader, explains that it is often necessary for people (in one or several of their lives) to do "evil" things, like killing, in order to learn invaluable spiritual lessons. She explains, "Our soul is saying, 'There is no good and evil. There are no victims. You are just experiencing this [killing people] so that you understand permission, so that you understand cosmic law." What a way to get an education! Not to worry though, says she, "victim and victimizer are one. . . . They are roles decided upon freely by all the players—agreed upon unanimously."[2] According to Griscom's belief, it is evidently true that rape victims (and all other victims) are "asking for it."

One of Griscom's more glamorous pupils, Shirley MacLaine, adds, "There is no such thing as a bad move, there is no such thing as a mistake. Everything is working to the purposeful good. I don't care if someone mugs me on the street; I drew it to myself."[3] Whoops! Sorry, Adolf Eichmann! We didn't understand that your slaughter of the Jews was not a "bad move." We failed to realize you were working to the purposeful good. Excuse us, please, Ku Klux Klansmen. I now realize that the Jews and blacks drew the hatred, beatings, and hangings to themselves. Forgive us, Charles Manson, for we knew not what we did.

In another vein, early gnostics, who troubled the church with their heresies, claimed that the only thing that was important was the soul. The foundation of their teaching was not in the Bible but Plato. They claimed that the body did not count and may do as it pleased, so long as the soul was given to God. In fact, they said, if our bodies do evil, that merely allows God's righteousness to shine more brightly. This was precisely the heresy that Paul the apostle addressed when he related that he had been falsely accused of saying, "Let us do evil that good may come." Still others claimed that following through on evil impulses would burn them out of their system, and they would emerge without the evil drive. Tantric yoga teaches this way and is practiced widely in the West. The same philosophy shines through the secular guise of the pseudo-scientific satiation or catharsis theories where an overdose of, say, pornography, will satiate perverse sexual drives and allow the person to not "act out" the perversion.

Complete secularists claim that good and evil are subject to the needs of mankind at the moment and, so, are transitory. One favorite is to say that homosexuality may have been correctly seen as wrong in times when increases in population were *needed*, but now that overpopulation is a problem, homosexuality, because it is barren, is a *positive good.*

The implication that to be like God, one must experience both good and evil, also questions God's righteousness. If He is intimately and experientially acquainted with both good and evil, then He is not all good. If God is not all good, then He could (and He later would) be blamed for the evil and troubles in man's world. Good and evil become an illusion, or at best, transitory ideas. In Eastern thought this is expressed in the common ejaculation, "It is all one"—good and evil are all the same thing. In modern movies like *Star Wars*, Western-Hindu scriptwriters write of "the light and dark sides of the Force"— but, they say, there is only one Force. Another movie, *Legend,* tells the tale of a good lad who rescues his love from an evil demon, a demon who will die at the touch of sunlight. The young man designs a method to bring the sunlight into the demon's dark, fiery lair. When he does, the demon, in the midst of his own destruction, laughs at the young man and foists his final lie. "You think you have won," he roars. "What is light without dark? I am a part of you all. You can never defeat me, we are brothers eternal."

In other words, light and dark, good and evil, are all one.

"God is all and *in all,*" the lie reverberates, "and God is in *you.*"

Blurring the Lines

"Woe to those who call evil good, and good evil; who substitute darkness for light and light for darkness; who substitute bitter for sweet, and sweet for bitter! Woe to those who are wise in their own eyes, and clever in their own sight."[4] It may seem almost silly that God would put such a thing in His Word, but even a superficial look at American culture will make His reason clear. Not that America has some kind of edge on this. Pagan societies throughout history have been the target of this woe. Many a sunken society has fallen to the "know good and evil" lie.

Perhaps the Serpent implied to Eve that God knew—in the sense of experiencing—all good and evil, a slanderous accusation. But all the same, Eve apparently was convinced that *she* needed to experience both. In fact, her hoped-for godhood, according to the Serpent, *depended* on her experiencing both. This philosophy still exists in Tantric Yoga.

All of this [occult paraphernalia and practices] is interwoven with antinomian practices, for the Tantric places himself above the conventional law. What others condemn, he assumes as a badge of nobility. What poisons others, nourishes him. What sends the herd to hell, ensures his salvation. Hence prohibited acts are used as rungs of the ladder by which he ascends to the heights.[5]

This version of the lie actually makes the doing of evil a stepping-stone to fulfillment. Naturally, most people will ask, "How many Tantrics are there? Are they a significant majority?" My answer is simple: "A Tantric, by any other name . . ." In other words, tantric beliefs held under other names are nonetheless tantric.

Take, for instance, the modern psychologist who encourages his patient to vent his anger. Is he not telling this person that his salvation is in allowing his anger to suffuse his entire being and that self-control will come from surrender to compulsiveness? What of the counselor who seeks to help the sex-offending pervert overcome his rudderless desires by showing him pornography? Is this not purity through putrefaction? Is this not Tantric thought in Western secular garb?

My own counseling experience tells me that those who practice "venting" anger become angrier and less controlled. Likewise, pornography may *temporarily* slake a sexual appetite, but later it is back with twice the power. Giving in to sin only makes it easier to give in to sin. Yet these practices are common even in church counseling circles, and they all fall under the now discredited catharsis or satiation theories.[6]

A slight variant on this idea says that one cannot know what is good and what is evil unless one expriences it. The saying in my youth was, "Don't knock it till you've tried it." This childish taunt has been echoed under the more sophisticated auspices of the "arts" community lately when they denounced believers who objected to the blasphemous (and incredibly boring[7]) movie, *The Last Temptation of Christ.* Pastors and congregations were chided by the media because they had not bothered to spend good money to see Christ portrayed as a sex pervert before "passing judgment" on the movie's merits. Two years later, when artists were presenting pictures of Jesus Christ immersed in urine and photos of explicit homosexual sex as government funded "art," objectors were told that they could not judge the "art" unless they first went to see the swill. In both of these cases, however, there were always enough "open-minded" clergy who found "merit" in the slanderous exhibitions for the fawning media to quote. No wonder that when the church speaks, nobody listens.

Jeremiah 15:19 says clearly, "Therefore, thus says the LORD, 'If you return, then I will restore you—before Me you will stand; and if you *extract the precious from the worthless* [the vile (KJV)], you will become My spokesman.' "

The Loss of Objective Truth

The Vanishing Ethic

"Now you see it," the black-tuxedoed magician said as he held the moral standard in the air. "And now you don't!" he added as the ethic disappeared.

"The mouth is quicker than the mind," he continued. "The lips passeth by all understanding."

Suddenly, a new ethic replaced the one that had just vanished. But this one was different—in fact, it was continually different. It changed with every passing second, with every shift in focus, situation, or point of view.

The magician bowed slightly and held it aloft. "Presenting: Situation Ethics," he said.

ᨵ ᨵ ᨵ

Situation ethics, popularized in our times in a book of that name by Dr. Joseph Fletcher, is an ancient ploy. The idea is that what is right is entirely dependent on each situation. Whatever causes the least misery for the fewest people is the right choice—or, to say it in a positive way, the decision which does the most good for the most people is right. That may have an appealing ring until you consider that each person involved in a given situation may have a completely *different* idea of what is best for most. Imagine the entire U.S. population of 250 million each believing in his or her own floating concepts of right and wrong. It would be—and is becoming—anarchy. What then? Do we revert to the law of the jungle and allow the strongest to decide? Might makes right? The divine right of kings?

There is a more distinctly self-centered version in which the individual decides what is right by what is best for him. This is actually the most common form of decision making among human beings, but few will openly admit it. Most prefer to have someone else, preferably a professional, help them make selfish decisions. Psychologists are good for this. You can always find a psychologist who will recommend what you already want to do as therapy "for your own good," and then encourage you to blame the doing on your parents, teachers, or other safely distant antagonists.[8]

In other words, what might be considered a sinful action is now justified by the fact that it may be good therapy. A perfect example is the misnomer, "therapeutic abortion." An abortion is therapy? The pro-abortion troops think so and want free access to child-killing as "therapy" for the mother. Yet the pro-aborts reject any suggestions that the mother be informed about the development of her baby because it might make her feel guilty about what she is doing.

The church is not free from blame either. If you have ever counseled a troubled believer, you have probably heard it. When you have delivered the plain Word of God to the situation the reply has been, "But you don't understand. My situation is *different*." That whine is the essence of situation ethics. Be it ever so lofty in presentation, though it is spoken by Nobel Prize winners, it still remains a childish excuse for sin.

Through the counseling field, situation ethics has invaded the church. Slick words and emotionally appealing arguments excuse sin as being a product of past abuses and traumas. Long sessions of self-pity and blaming others are engendered and excused as necessary for the person's "inner healing" and recovering self-esteem. The "sufferer" is not held responsible for his homosexuality (or drunkenness, drug use, uncontrollable temper, promiscuity) because he is just "acting out hurts" from long ago. Other times, it is said that a man has a wife who simply "doesn't understand" him or "fulfil his needs." On the opposite end, a woman who has a husband who commits the ultimate sin of "insensitivity." Most Christian psychologists, as well as others, affix the blame for all of these things on low self-esteem, which in turn is caused by trauma and abuse. My question, like that of the agnostic psychologist who wrote a book on the subject, is, "Whatever happened to sin?"

Whether it is in humanistic philosophy or baptized psychology, situation ethics usurps God's role as the ultimate arbiter of good and evil. Man replaces God, or perhaps makes himself God's equal.

Evolving Ethics

"The Constitution is a *living* document," they tell you. "It was intended to grow and develop along with society and to change with society's changing needs and mores."

This is the American legal version of situation ethics. The constitution does not actually *mean* anything, they say, it only means what we *need* it to mean at the moment. This free-floating law is called *legal positivism*. Those in power decide what the country needs and interpret the laws and constitution to facilitate those needs. Both courts and legislatures make sociological law based on their assessment of what is right and wrong, and that assessment can change without notice when the leaders see a need for change. Thus, unconstitutional decisions such as the *Roe v. Wade* abortion decision are possible.

In ancient times tyrants ruled for their own pleasure. Today, they do the same, only they make the pretense that it is for "the common good." An example is when the U.S. Congress passed a law in 1989 requiring government agencies and businesses who deal with the government to hire women and minorities. But they exempted congressional staffs from the mandate. The attitude is clearly reflected by the liberal icon, former U.S. Supreme Court Justice Oliver Wendell Holmes.

> "Truth," Holmes said, "[is] the majority vote of that nation that could lick all others." He declared that "when it comes to the development of a *corpus juris* [body of law] the ultimate question is what do the dominant forces of the community want and do they want it hard enough to disregard whatever inhibitions stand in the way."[9]

Evidently, in the case of abortion, someone (or some seven) "wanted it hard enough." Sorry, kids!

But note the strict evolutionary character of this belief. It is truly survival-of-the-fittest—the fittest being those "dominant forces" who can "lick all others." Most people are naive enough to believe that laws are being changed to fit current realities. The truth is that law is changed to fit the pleasures and plans of the powerful "fittest" in the upper stratum of society. The politically weak or holders of minority opinions are squeezed into extinction as the strong "disregard whatever inhibitions stand in the way."

Still, evolving law is not usually presented with visions of cruel, survival-of-the-fittest panoramas. This is especially true among those who try to coerce Biblical morality to evolve. Many modern theologians claim that the prohibitions of the Old Testament, such as those against homosexuality, were suited only to that ancient, agrarian culture and do not apply to more urban societies like our own. Others say that, like manners, morals change from society to society and that we should try to see how we can adapt the Word of God to the culture. Maybe they thought Jesus told us to "Go therefore and become disciples of all nations, learning from them all the wisdom that their cultures have to offer."

The entire concept of evolution itself, much less moral or legal evolution, is flawed from the outset. The evolution of species, especially man, rules out the fallen nature of man and thus his need for salvation. The irrational belief that man, society, laws, and everything else are on a continuous upward spiral has no basis in historical fact. Barbarity is always at the gates and is repelled only with great effort, but now the chief barbarian is in our midst—evolution.

Personalized Ethics

"Start your own religion," advised psychedelic guru Timothy Leary back in the 1960s—and most people have. In fact most people have *always* had their own religion. Paganism allows that. Privatized faith is very convenient—and very American. Billions have bought their private sets of commandments and done what seemed right to them. Even in Christian circles, it seems, the watchword is "Your truth is your truth. My truth is my truth."

Atheists, if they are honest, will admit that without God there is no ultimate authority except each individual's will. Polytheists, with their all-too-human, whimsical gods, have no basis for morality either, since their gods have no morality. Humanists may point to "the good of mankind" as their ethical source, though what is or isn't good is still up to changeable man. All of these, however, have one thing in common—they have to make their own rules about right and wrong.

How many times have you been told that only *you know what is right for you*? It is a popular truism (this does not mean it is true, only that it appears true). And certainly, those who give this counsel honestly believe there is no objective standard of behavior.

Corrie Ten Boom used to tell the story of the telephone operator who received a daily call from a man inquiring about the time. This call came at just about noon every day. Her curiosity aroused, she asked the man why he called daily at noon needing the time. He explained, "I am responsible to blow the factory whistle at noon and I am just insuring that I am on time."

The operator gasped. "But," she replied, "I set my watch by that whistle."

As the illustration shows, without an objective standard, one could get quite a ways off before the error would become evident. Of course, those who teach that each man is a law unto himself believe that there are limitations to that concept, but it is always *their* limitations. Who is to say that *their* limitations should have priority over other people's choice of boundaries? You see how messy all of this becomes without an outside standard. This is precisely the confusion that has swallowed Western society and which has seriously infiltrated the church. Biblical scholars are questioning everything from the creation to the return of Christ, from the Biblical call to holiness to the warnings about sin. Afraid of taking a firm stand, they retreat to saying that each man must relate to God in his or her own way. For example, consider the degeneracy of the Alcoholics Anonymous creed. AA originally began with a real belief in and dependence upon the God of the Bible and descended to one which tells people to rely upon "God, whatever they conceive him to be." That last qualification is very important because in the AA meetings, God, or the Higher Power, can be Jesus, your inner self, the doorknob, or anything else you choose. I recall listening to a woman who was an adherent of Narcotics Anonymous (NA), a twelve-step group based on the AA doctrines, who spoke of how, five years before, her Higher Power had told her that it was wrong to continue to smoke marijuana. However, she explained, her Higher Power had now told her it was no problem to use pot. Evidently, *her* Higher Power cannot make up its mind.

Part of the original Protestant rejection of the Roman church's authority revolved around the question of who read and interpreted the Bible. The reformers claimed that the Holy Spirit was given to all believers, in part, to interpret the Scriptures to them. Therefore, they argued, the ordinary believer ought to have access to a Bible. Rome vigorously disagreed. They felt that only trained theologians were capable of interpreting the Word. While the reformers were right about their assertion, many today seem to believe that Luther and others fought for the right of "personal interpretation" of the Bible. Nothing could be further from the truth. The reformers were quite aware of 2 Peter 1:20—"But know this first of all, that no prophecy of Scripture is a matter of one's own interpretation."

Yet, many believers today think that it is their inalienable right to draw whatever conclusions from the Word of God that suit their fancy. I recall once confronting a false teacher at an informal church gathering in the early 1970s who was explaining to some new believers how the Scripture permitted the use of marijuana. I clearly denounced the teaching before the little group, to the horrified looks of some of the believers who felt I was not being "loving." He began to argue his point, so I invited him to preach his phony "gospel" somewhere off the church property. I insisted that he could not preach such falsehood in the church building while I was around.

Suddenly, up came a young man who must have felt he was acting the role of "peacemaker." He tried to conciliate our disagreement by saying, "Wait a minute, brothers! Suppose that the Holy Spirit has revealed to this brother (indicating me) that smoking pot is a sin and to this brother (indicating our heretical friend) that smoking pot is not a sin . . ."

I looked at the erstwhile peacemaker in utter disbelief. A look of realization crossed his face and he stopped mid-sentence. Next, I ran the unrepentant false prophet off the property. But I had members of that church angry with me for weeks over what I had done. They felt that this guy had a right to interpret Scripture the way he did.

What has happened in the American church is that the great doctrine of the priesthood of all believers has been distorted. Instead of each man receiving what God gives by the Holy Spirit, it has become each man receiving what he wants from his own spirit. But the clear warning of Scripture is against every man doing what is right in his own eyes (see Deuteronomy 12:8). The church is being paganized.

If there ever was a capsule description of paganism, this passage in Deuteronomy is it. The pagan revivalists in America say that the only law is, "Harming none, do what you will." Naturally, it is up to the individual to decide what is "harming none." Aleister Crowley, a turn-of-the-century warlock (a practitioner of early European paganism), is more honest in his prime directive. He merely says, "Do what you will."

But the "personal interpretation" beliefs in the church today mirror—in result, at least—the same pagan ideology, despite the ominous warning of Proverbs 16:25, "There is a way which seems right to a man, but its end is the way of death."

There Are Absolutely No Absolutes

Do you believe in traditional family values? I would venture that most of you do. But perhaps you are unaware of how such a belief undermines true moral character.

If this statement puzzles you, allow me to make this point: Not only do ideas have consequences, but ideas can be conveyed *and subverted* by words. The old debater's axiom comes into play—He who frames the question, wins the debate. And in this case, the hidden reef that sinks our ideological ship is the term *values*. When we discuss "values" it signifies that a thing is only valuable to the degree that you, as an individual, value it. "Values" are subject to change. For instance, gold's value changes on the world market day by day, minute by minute. The price of oil has one value on the "spot" market and another elsewhere.

But there used to be a gold standard, just as there used to be a moral standard. The price of gold (and morality) was fixed—a constant. These were standards against which all things were measured. Today the value of chastity on the "spot" market is very low, and lower yet in all other markets. The "value" of marriage is only high if it is the right *kind* of marriage, i.e., one where each partner feels fulfilled, where each is free to "grow" as a person. No longer is it important for man and woman to surrender individuality to obtain the unity of marriage. Marriage is now two people living apart together. But the standard of marriage was "till death do us part." Of course, this was back when keeping a vow was also a standard.

Values are mere trinkets to be changed at a whim. This year I value my financial status, next year I will value my relationships or my being "sensitive"—whatever is more trendy. Standards are established, like the boundary stones of ancient Israel that God forbade the Israelites to move.

So the acceptance of the term *values* in place of *standards* signals our defection from the absolutes of right and wrong. The idea that there are no absolutes (which is an absolute in itself) has spawned the bastard truism, "You can't legislate morality." The presumption is that there is no such thing as morality—that it varies from person to person, from day to day. Morality is completely arbitrary and personal and, therefore, cannot be properly codified into law.

Such a conclusion is obviously insane unless morals are merely personal preferences, but we act upon that erroneous judgment daily. We presume to negotiate elastic bounds for good and evil when God has clearly created a line between the two. One way to fleece this wolf of the artificial sheepskin of values is to consciously replace it with the term *preference*. Here are some practice phrases for you:

- The new curriculum is designed to teach children moral values in a nonreligious way.

- Most Americans claim to have strong religious values.

- The candidate said he believed in traditional family values.

Clearly, there is a difference between the perceived meaning of the above sentences and their true meaning as seen with the word *preferences* substituted for *values*. When someone has "religious preferences" it means that he prefers his own ideas on religion, whatever they may be, to those of others. But when he is said to have "religious values" it *sounds like* he has adopted the overriding moral code of a particular religion.

The two should not be confused. The statement that he has values does not mean that he has standards.

The Fruit of the Spirit Is *Not* Tolerance

Why, then, do so many current sages tell us that "evil" and "good" are just subjective, arbitrary opinions?

The answer may lie in an ideological disease that seems to afflict democracies throughout history. You might call it pseudoegalitarianism, but I prefer to call it "bastard pluralism." (That shocks people into listening carefully.)

> In a democracy we say, "Everyone is entitled to his
> opinion," but then some people jump from this to the
> unjustified conclusion: "Everyone's opinion is right."[10]

The author of the above quote correctly analyzed the
dissolution of good and evil in our society. The highest
virtue today appears to be tolerance, even tolerance of
outright lies. Today, tolerance means that all beliefs, no
matter how bizarre, are of equal value and deserving of
equal respect. Naturally, if this is true there cannot be any
absolutes of right and wrong. But among the tolerance
promoters there is one thing that they *will not tolerate*—
that is intolerance. So long as Christians say that Jesus is *a*
way, they are tolerated. The moment believers proclaim
the gospel that Jesus is *the* Way, they cannot be tolerated.
They absolutely will not tolerate absolutes. Early Christians were constantly in trouble over this.

> Narrow indeed was the gate that admitted into the new
> Society, and broad that of admission into other religions.
> In the matter of intolerance Christianity differed from
> all pagan religions, and surpassed Judaism; in that re-
> spect it stood in direct opposition to the spirit of the
> age. It was emphatic in its positive differential doctrines
> and uncompromising in its stern protests: it had "inher-
> ited from Judaism the courage of its disbeliefs." Never
> was there a more tolerant age than that into which
> Christianity appeared. . . . Racial and religious barriers
> had been thrown down. . . . Men were everywhere ex-
> changing religious views. Syncretism was the religious
> hallmark of the time. Throughout the empire were
> spreading religious communities in which men of differ-
> ent races met. There was no clear line of demarcation
> among the foreign cults, which showed a marked hospi-
> tality in religion. Different gods agreed to be housed in
> the same temple; the same priest might officiate for half
> a dozen deities. Men were willing to try every religion

and philosophy in the field. It was now as fashionable to owe allegiance to the gods of the Nile, Syria, Persia, Samothrace, Greece, and Rome, as it had been in the previous epoch to acknowledge only one national pantheon. Polytheism is naturally tolerant, and the spirit of the age only increased religious tolerance. . . .

But we shall less regret this intolerance of primitive Christianity when we reflect upon the nature and necessity of it. . . . Tolerance too often results from indifference or indecision, but the intolerance of the Christian preachers was that of the conviction that they had found *the* all-comprehensive Truth. And in the welter of religions and philosophies intolerance was the most obvious, if not also the only sure, method of self-preservation. . . . Greek thought, on the other side, saw in Christianity immense possibilities of speculation and essayed to transform it into an eclectic philosophy in which the metaphysical would predominate over the spiritual. Again, the Mysteries, with their numerous clientele, welcomed Christianity as another religion of their own genus, offering hospitality to its Christ and to its rites. But the Holy Spirit, as the Christians termed the new source of power which they felt better than they could describe, warned the "new way" of the perils of holding dalliance with other cults. The event [the fall of Rome] justified them. The hospitality and syncretism of the competitors of Christianity, while greatly adding to their popularity, ultimately compassed their downfall.[11]

Could there be any better description of our American pluralism? And could there be any worse description of today's Christian response to this dissolution of good and evil?

If someone believes that God has given absolute standards to man and that these standards are good for him, he must attempt to fashion society with these morals. In other words, he must commit the worst crime of the twentieth century—he must "impose his morality" on others. The alternative is to have the "do what you will" pagan path of (almost) universal tolerance *imposed on you.*

Review

The seventh lie, "knowing good and evil," may be rendered as:

- You must experience good and evil.
- You can decide for yourself what is good and evil.
- Good and evil are an illusion.
- God is both good and evil.
- Good and evil are two sides of the same coin.
- Good and evil are subjective.
- Good and evil are situational.
- Good and evil are transitory.
- Good and evil are nonexistent.
- There are no absolutes.

N I N E

THE WHY OF THE LIE

The Bible tells us the truth about God and the truth about man," Billy Graham once said. And we turn now to the Word of God to answer an important question: Why do lies work?

One would think after thousands of years of failure from believing lies, man would learn to stop blindly accepting them—at least *some* of them. But man persists in ramming his head against the walls of truth, trying to live out his delusion that there are no walls. What is it that draws humanity, moth-like, toward the flames of hell in utter defiance of God's easily demonstrated truth?

In the past chapters we have looked at the seven basic lies of Satan. In review, they were:

1. Hath God said . . . ?
2. You shall not eat of every tree in the Garden?
3. You shall surely not die.
4. For God doth know that in the day that you eat thereof . . .
5. Your eyes shall be opened.

6. You shall be as gods.

7. Knowing good and evil.

They appear to be such simple little lies, but they wear so many masks. You have probably thought, as I have inferred throughout this book, that these lies are best suited to work as teams. For instance, someone may think this way: "There is no God (1). So that means man is at the top (6) and he can make the rules (7)." Or perhaps he says to himself, "Is God really against (1) our living together (2)? We love each other so much that He would have to be against true love to object (4)." The answer to why these work year after year and century after century is in the Bible.

Men Lo'e the Mirk and No the Licht

This is how they read John 3:19 in Scotland.[1] In colonial English it is, "Men loved the darkness rather than the light." Why? The passage continues, "For their deeds were evil." Man is basically wicked, but he wants no one to know it so he cloaks his true nature in darkness. And that hiding is also part of the corrupt human nature. Why else would it be so hard for people to say those three simple words, "I have sinned," which would lead to their forgiveness and salvation?

There is no truth so neglected and yet so necessary to man's understanding of himself as the doctrine of man's fallen and depraved nature. Self-esteem teachings notwithstanding, man *deserves* a poor self-image. He is a poor self! In truth, he deserves death and damnation. Until this fact is recognized and taken into account, mankind will go blundering along thinking that their instincts can be trusted. And calamity will always follow.

Men's fallen natures "lo'e the mirk," as the Scots say. Even when man tries to do good, he falls short of God's righteous requirement. But if man is not fallen, he needs no Christ. God has so constructed creation that it reflects His perfect and holy character. Sin has no place in God's presence and His justice demands retribution for sin. But God's mercy made it possible for man to escape this horrible retribution and still maintain God's justice.

Mankind, however, has a great talent as an escape artist—a talent first exercised by Adam when he hid himself from God and sewed fig leaves together to cover his nakedness. When discovered, he immediately began to play psychic hide-and-seek. "*She* did it!" he cried.

The incident is our first look at another kind of lie—self-delusion. Man doesn't need Satan to feed him a line. If necessary, he will lie to himself! Modern professional psychologists call this phenomena "denial," which covers everything from seeing one's own personal faults, the faults of loved ones, symptoms of one's own mortality, or the truth about the corrupt nature of man. But the psychologists themselves are "in denial" about that last one.

At this point you might say, "I can understand the carnal nature inclining people toward sin, but Adam and Eve were perfect, weren't they? Why would they sin?"

This is a good question and, as always, the Scripture gives us an answer.

A Tale of Three Foes

"For all that is in the world and the lust of the flesh, the lust of the eyes and the boastful pride of life, is not from the Father, but is from the world" (1 John 2:16). The Scripture points to three enemies of man's soul: the world, the flesh, and the devil. Of these three I believe the most deadly is the flesh—the enemy within. The world may lure and the devil may coax, but the flesh drives. The man himself must voluntarily surrender for sin to be complete.

The above verse in 1 John indicates that there are three footholds in a man where temptation may take hold: lust of the flesh, lust of the eyes, and the pride of life. We see these in Eve's temptation. The lust of the flesh may encompass any physical, emotional, or intellectual needs that seek satisfaction outside of God's design—gluttony, sex outside of marriage, close friendships with people who entice you away from Christ, knowledge gained from divination or other prohibited sources, and any number of other fleshly drives. The lust of the eyes is fairly obvious. Envy, covetousness, and other illicit desires whose chief link is eyesight are all covered. The pride of life consists mostly of the subliminal thought, "I live, therefore, I do what I want." It is the choice of the self-will over submission to God's and involves not just pride, as in haughtiness, but pride and independence. The phrase with which you are no doubt familiar and that best sums it up is, "Whose life is it, anyway?"

But you are still wondering about the innocence of the first couple.

Yes, Eve was perfect and, as yet, innocent. But Eve was not perfect in the sense that Christ is. She did have capabilities of choice and had not yet chosen good or evil. Christ's choice was made when He obeyed the Father in becoming incarnate. Scripture does not inform us what Eve was doing near the tree, but it does tell us the state of mind she was in when she plucked the fruit from the branch.

"When the woman saw that the tree was good for food, and that it was a delight to the eyes, and that the tree was desirable to make one wise, she took from its fruit and ate."[2] Curiously, the words "pleasing to the sight and good for food" are used to describe *all* the trees that God caused to grow in Eden (see Genesis 2:9). Alone, these aspects of the tree did not constitute a problem. Visual beauty and goodness of taste or nutrition in themselves were part of what God called good in His creation. It was certainly subtle of Satan to link his temptation of inordinate knowledge with an element of God-created good. A good contemporary example is how God created a good thing in the sexual experience of man and wife, but how it has been used as the lure to deceive people into seeking *inordinate* pleasure merely for the sake of pleasure.[3]

What I am saying is that temptation will most commonly be accompanied by some "good" that can be satisfied by surrender. The lure may simply be to indulge in an excess of a good thing. Just as too much good food is gluttony and too much attention to beauty is vanity, so a search for esoteric wisdom is presumption. Nevertheless, the skids will be liberally greased with platitudes and plaudits. The hidden voice will echo, "There's nothing *wrong* with pleasant food. In fact it's a blessing." And one can easily recall the promise of the 1960s drug movement —that drugs were "desirable to make one wise."

Also remember that Genesis instructs us that the tree of life *and* the forbidden tree were standing together "in the midst of the garden" (see Genesis 2:9). Eve might just as easily stepped over to the Tree of Life instead. And today, couples who live in sin might just as easily go get married. Many times our choices are this clear-cut.

As the name suggests Genesis is a book of beginnings, and this story of Eve's temptation was the beginning of man's fall. In Eve's state of mind, we see three of the powerful draws on man for sin.

- The lust of the flesh = she saw that the tree was good for food.

- The lust of the eyes = and that it was a delight to the eyes.

- The pride of life = and that the tree was desirable to make one wise.

A survey of Biblical stories of temptation will reveal these three are, separately or in tandem, integral to all sin. Think for a moment of the story of David and Bathsheba—a walk on the roof and a glance over the parapet. . . . To paraphrase, "He saw that the woman was a delight to the eyes and sexually exciting."

More to the point was the threefold temptation of our Lord in the wilderness (see Luke 4). Satan appeared to Jesus after forty days of fasting and the Scripture says, "He [Jesus] became hungry." So Satan's tack is, "Here, satisfy your hunger [appeal to the flesh]—after all, you *are* the Son of God [appeal to the pride]."

The attempt was flattened by Jesus so Satan moved on. "Well," he said, "Look at all these kingdoms I can give you [appeal to the eyes]. All you have to do is worship me."

But Jesus was not buying. Satan, however, persistent salesman that he is, was not through yet. "Show everyone your power [appeal to the pride]! Step off this pinnacle. You *know* you won't get hurt—the Bible even says so!"

Again, the temptation was foiled by Jesus who placed all His trust in the Father. *Later*, when it suited the Father's purpose, Jesus created food by multiplying loaves and fishes, not out of stone but out of air! *Later*, again when it was the Father's will, He showed everyone His power and proved His divinity when He rose from the dead. And *later* all the kingdoms of the world were assigned to Him.

But back to Eve. Though she was perfect, she was as yet not *perfected*. Adam and Eve needed to choose God of their own accord to achieve that state, and this was especially true for Eve, who was newly created after the naming of the animals. The Hebrew words for the naming implies more than calling them by a species but rather calling them by their attributes. The implication is that Eve may not have known that the Serpent was "more crafty" than the other beasts. That part is speculative, but a good probability since the New Testament tells us that Eve was tricked, and Adam, who obviously knew better, disobeyed deliberately.[4] The Word does not instruct us that by Eve's sin death was brought into the world, but by Adam's. His is the worse offense.

Eve's Disease

"What you don't know won't hurt you," he said stepping unknowingly into the path of the speeding eighteen-wheeler truck.

The Scripture, not to mention the eighteen-wheeler, would refute that popular proverb. The Bible says, "Therefore My people go into exile [captivity] for their lack of knowledge. . . . Therefore Sheol has enlarged its throat and opened its mouth without measure. . . ."[5] The truck simply says, "Thump-thump."

Eve's disease appears to have been ignorance. What she didn't know *did* hurt her—and everyone since. But ignorance can be from two sources. In Eve's case, as with new believers and other children, it was entirely understandable. This is why careful discipleship of new believers is so important. "Leading someone to the Lord" without any thought of follow-up is generally irresponsible. I say "generally" because there are cases where it is truly impossible to do so. But, as a rule, new believers should not be left to the winds of doctrine that blow every direction in today's society.

As these new disciples learn to search the Word carefully, they make themselves less vulnerable to deception. They become more aware of how God thinks. When they are then confronted with new ideas which are wrong, they will often sense or discern the "wrongness" even before they can articulate a scriptural response. "But solid food is for the mature, who *because of practice* have their senses trained to discern good and evil" (Hebrews 5:14, emphasis added). Their willingness to hear and do the Word acts as a lamp to light their way.[6]

The great danger of scriptural ignorance, no matter how produced, is that it creates ambiguity, uncertainty, and confusion about what is and is not true. The reason that this state of mind leaves a man particularly susceptible to a lie is that man has a natural drive for order and stability. His mind seeks out anchor points and will as easily latch onto a seemingly stable lie as the truth. *A good lie will replace uncertainty.* And the storm-tossed mind will be grateful for the chance to hold on to something that appears to be solid. Some of this is evidenced in the rapid growth of strong Bible churches, but there is also a comparable growth in all religions that have solid "truths" and clear do's and don't's. This is true even of cults whose beliefs are incredibly bizarre.

The second form of ignorance closely borders our earlier comments on the carnal nature. Men simply "lo'e the mirk." And this being so, they remain ignorant through apathy, laziness, or sloppiness. The apathetic simply consider knowing God and His Word as low priority; these may not even bother with getting any input other than their Sunday sermon.

As an example, I recently heard a tape of a woman teaching on abortion at a local church. The visiting speaker explained to the congregation that because God had given Adam and Eve a choice about disobeying Him, that this meant that freedom of choice was an ultimate value in God's eyes. Because of this, she explained, any attempt to legislate or pressure women not to have abortions was a violation of the sacred blessing of choice given by God. She was saying that a woman's decision to murder her own child was a sacred act! God may bless us with the *ability* to chose, but this does not mean He sanctifies our choices. What was more astonishing, though, was the response of the congregation. During the question and answer period there was no outrage, no challenge of her interpretation, and not one comment from the pastor. There were one or two muted—extremely muted—statements that sounded almost as though they could be construed as pro-life. The questions asked betrayed an appalling ignorance of the Word of God.

The lazy are similar. They leave all the Bible study to the "experts" and lean on what they say instead of checking out what they hear. In fact, many of these are constantly reading Christian books and listening to Bible study tapes, but they are usually swayed by rhetoric and "good preaching" rather than the commands of Scripture. Whether it is intellectual argument or emotional pitch that persuades them, the possibilities for "captivity" are great.

Sloppiness, on the other hand, can come from laziness but usually involves another motive. This person adopts a slap-dash approach. He "knows" what point he is looking to prove, but does not really want to do the homework to find verses that actually speak to the subject. Instead, it is easier to take verses that seem to fit the point than to spend time searching the Scriptures. But the habit of taking the easy verse may lead to error.

A common misuse of Scripture is the quoting of Revelation 3:20, "Behold I stand at the door and knock," as a call to the lost when it is clearly Christ *trying to get back into* His church. Certainly, Jesus *is* calling the lost and there are many verses to address that, but it is sheer laziness to lean on that verse—in many cases because it has a better "ring" for our sermons. This example is mere slovenliness. The meaning of the text could easily be broadened to include the lost, so it may seem that there is no great loss. However, I believe that sloppiness in using Scripture will, like all things, bear manifold fruit toward "captivity."

An example more pertinent to our subject is the scurrilous use of the alleged Scripture, "As a man thinketh in his heart, so is he," which finds nearly continuous trade among the positive thinking and the blab-it-and-grab-it crowds. The verse itself, Proverbs 23:7, is normally mangled from the King James Version and actually says, "For as *he* thinketh in his heart, so is he." The *he* in this case is an evil, envious, selfish man—whom you are being warned to avoid because *he* has *thoughts* that *he thinketh in his heart* about you. They are not thoughts of how to bless you tenfold, either. Yet I have heard the supposedly most Biblically sound preachers and teachers use this verse to promote positive thinking. This, even from those who do not preach the "power" aspects of this kind of thinking.

Some of these verses are simply crutches to prop our unwillingness to find out what Scripture actually says as opposed to what we are planning to say in our next message. Eventually these verses become nearly proverbial within the church culture. Sometimes, as with my first example, the meaning could have broad applicability to a teaching that actually is true. Other times, it slides over into teachings that are questionable at best and heresy at worst. It all depends on where you start. Think for a moment of the possibilities if someone *begins* with the wrong teaching. My second example will serve well here. This abuse of God's Word is one of the reasons why people believe that one may "prove anything they want from the Bible." Clearly people should take ideas and submit them to the Word of God rather than looking for proof within the Scriptures for their own prefabricated points.

The Scripture clearly admonishes us to,

> Make your ear attentive to wisdom, incline your heart to understanding; for if you cry for discernment, lift your voice for understanding; if you seek her as silver, and search for her as for hidden treasures; then you will discern the fear of the LORD, and discover the knowledge of God. (Proverbs 2:2–5)

A Bite from Adam's Apple

I had only been sovereignly saved for a couple of months and had just started to go to a church; in fact, this was my first church service. It was a cool California evening outside Calvary Chapel after the meeting, and I was talking to another of the Christian refugees from the hippie culture.

"I guess I'd better get home," I told him. "I'm kind of tired and I'd like to smoke a joint and go to bed."

A puzzled expression crossed the other's face. "You still smoke pot?" he queried.

"Sure. Nothin' wrong with that. It's natural—one of the plants God put here."

"Well, brother," he said shaking his head, "the Bible tells us that we should obey the laws of the land—it doesn't honor Jesus to do that."

I stammered and argued that it was a bad law and that it was alright to ignore a bad law. The other just reiterated, "Well, that's what the Bible *says*, man." In my mind I argued all the way home. But when I lit the joint I was suddenly struck by the simplicity of the truth that the man had spoken. I flushed the rest of my pot down the toilet.

Another friend, who stood with me during the initial argument, came home with me, lit the joint with me, and watched the small stash go whirling down the drain. But he later made a choice to disobey and reject God's deliverance, and he was ever after on a roller-coaster of spirituality and sensuality, never quite able to escape the jaws of sin.

I shudder to think about it. I *know* how easily I could have made the same choice.

Deliberate disobedience; willing deception; a hardheaded choice to depart from God which results in slavery to sin and leads to death itself—no condition is more common to human beings than this "nature of Adam" that permeates us all. The rebellious Adam lives, breathes, and animates everyone born human. In Christ, this carnal man is dealt a death blow and a "new creature in Christ" is born.

But the babe must be nurtured and given time to grow. And though the "old man" has been delivered unto death, its rotting corpse seems intent on resurrection and a *coup*. In the middle stands the will—the power of free choice given to every believer by the Spirit which allows him to actually choose to follow God. Before, sin was ever the master; now, the believer cannot be *forced* back into slavery. He can, however, choose to serve his old master for his old wages.

For a Christian to believe that he cannot be freed from the power of sin is to deny the effectiveness of the grace and blood of Jesus Christ. But to believe that Christians are no longer able to be completely overcome by the carnal nature is to invite disaster.

A former pastor of mine used to say, "If a man knows his own spirit, he will not be deceived by flattery." This is especially true if that flatterer implies that you can no longer fall into sin. Man is *always* ready to believe what sounds good to his ears. A good example is found in today's public school system. Despite continuously falling public school test scores (on tests that have been seriously "dumbed down"), deliberately overlooking reports of students who cannot identify their own state on a map, and ignoring high school graduates who read at second and third grade levels, American teachers still tell their students that they are the most intelligent, best educated young people that the world has yet produced (I was told this same flattering balderdash as well when I was in school). What is remarkable is that the teachers actually believe it. And what bodes more evil for the future is that the haughty little illiterates in the classroom answer that they knew it all along. For the students, the news is not news; it merely confirms their arrogant self-appraisal. Man is quite capable of successfully believing a lie about himself, especially if it panders to pride. Here, the teachers *want* to believe that their methods are right and successful. This is similar to the scientist whose tests on mice disprove his theory so he disposes of the mice and deems them defective. Despite the evidence, he believes what he believes because *he wants to believe it*.

Direct disobedience may also hide itself behind a mask of self-deception. In this instance lying to oneself consists of *knowing* what God says and wants, then choosing some other way. But even true ignorance does not excuse one from responsibility. In the Old Covenant there were specifically prescribed sacrifices for sins committed in ignorance; there was still a price to pay (see Numbers 15:22–29).

Jesus said, "That slave who knew his master's will and did not get ready or act in accord with his will, shall receive many lashes, but the one who did not know it, and committed deeds worthy of a flogging, will receive but few" (Luke 12:47–48). Ignorance for those who have known Christ for years is inexcusable. In this country Bibles, concordances, lexicons, dictionaries, and excellent cross-reference materials are freely available. I declare that we will face the judgment seat of Christ and be measured by this standard: "And from everyone who has been given much, shall much be required; and to whom they entrusted much, of him they will ask all the more" (v. 48).

Review

In this chapter we've concluded that:

- Lies work.
- They work because men love darkness rather than light.
- Man has three enemies: the world, the flesh, and the devil.
- The flesh is deadliest because it is involved in all sins of man.

- The flesh has three strong points of temptation: the lust of the flesh, the lust of the eyes, and the pride of life.

- One may fall to temptation by deception (as Eve) or by disobedience (as Adam).

- Deception can be due to ignorance, apathy, laziness, or willful ignorance.

- Disobedience may be either defiant or the result of self-deception.

- Until we are changed into Christ's image at His return, we will always have to be vigilant against our carnal nature.

- Ignorance is no excuse, and willful ignorance is rebellion.

- To whom much is given, much will be required.

TEN

A STAR
TO STEER HER BY

You walk through the church looking at its structure. You are amazed by the diversity of style and workmanship—none of it seems to fit and yet none is entirely out of place. Somehow, most of it seems to hang together within the original frame despite the differences.

But in your survey, you step on a slick spot of self-esteem spilled on the floor that causes you to lose your balance and change your direction. You wonder who left that lying around. Curiously, the slick is located near a new wing of the church—a wing adding another section to the original framework. In fact, workers from the Humanists Co., who are constructing the wing, are busily at it today. Dust from their work seems to pervade most of the building, getting in your eyes and blurring your vision.

Another thing that invades the peace and quiet of your inspection is the background music from the newly installed P.A. system which sings sweetly, if repetitively, "Nearer, My Self, to Thee." You find yourself humming the compelling tune.

When you arrive at the basement, you find to your dismay that some of the stones have been removed and replaced by large blocks of evolutionary plaster . . .

෪ ෪ ෪

The twentieth-century church seems adrift in a sea of uncertainty in need of "a star to steer her by," as the poet said. The original poem's character claims he is the "captain" of his soul and his destiny—such egoism has no place in the church. But both share the need for the guiding "star." In the poem, *he* is the star of his own choice; with the church, the guide is the Word of God.

Even though Christ is the head of the church, the church can choose to steer herself. Jesus may be the head of the church, but He obviously does not exert absolute control. I cannot imagine that our Lord would have piloted the church into the Sargasso Sea in which we are mired. Instead, the church seems to set its course on Jesus *and* something else, rather like the recommended temptation in C. S. Lewis's *Screwtape Letters* where the elder devil advises the younger to get his "patient" (the Christian) to fall for mixing something else with his faith. He called it the "Christianity *and* . . ." temptation. It is as though believers, especially highly respected ones, are embarrassed to rely solely on God's Word. They blanch at the accusation that they might be Bible *literalists*.

But as Dr. Dow Pursley once put it, "Not too many years from now, if the Lord tarries, I will die and then appear before the judgment seat of Christ. I have determined on that great day I would rather have the Lord say to me, 'Dow, you took My Word too literally,' than for Him to say, 'Dow, you took My precious Word and explained it all away.' "[1]

You *Can* Go Home

Remember the exhilaration and the wonder when you first knew Christ? Do you recall your first reading of the Word after you received the Spirit of God to open your eyes—how every word stood out, and you were amazed and marveled at the pure and simple message? How you drank in every syllable like a thirsty man and treasured each phrase?

What happened? Did the intellectual aspects of the Word that were "desirable to make one wise" draw you away from the simplicity of the truth? Perhaps, when you began to see God's Word with its layers of meaning, you abandoned the straight meaning of the text as unnecessary—or maybe even "unintellectual." Soon, the symbolic had more meaning than the actual words. When you read, "Feed the hungry," you saw "Give people spiritual food—Bibles," and you ignored the struggling family in your own church even when the breadwinner was laid off.

It didn't happen all at once. The enticing lure of the so-called deep things of God slowly replaced the "shallow" things, such as childlike faith, prayer, and the unabashed presentation of the truth of Scripture. But the joy was gone. The adventure of *knowing God* became a fevered pursuit of the intricacies of knowledge *about* Him. You used to believe *every word* He said; now you are not so sure. Well-known Bible teachers tell you that such doubts are a sign of maturity. The boundaries faded as the clear statements of Scripture were submerged—lost beneath the sea of types, shadows, and allegories. Deep inside, you knew something important was gone, but you couldn't say just *what*.

You want to go home.

A voice echoes, "I have this against you, that you have left your first love. Remember therefore from where you have fallen, and repent and do the deeds you did at first."[2]

❧   ❧   ❧

The first step in returning from the murky confusion of lies is to acknowledge your condition—murky and confused. First John 1:9 tells us that forgiveness and cleansing come when we confess our sins to Him. And what greater sin is there than refusal to believe God's Word. After all, the one sin from which no one recovers is failing to believe the Word's claim that Christ's death saves you from hell.

But the journey does not end there. Your childhood in faith, much like the one in the natural, provided unrepeatable experiences. These must give way to more mature practice. Where, in youth, instant confirmations of God's truth abounded, slowly God began exercising you in taking His Word by faith alone. Somehow you skipped these lessons while on your intellectual side trip. You will have to learn that all-important, implicit trust, and it may be difficult at this late stage. You must return to the plain Word. Nothing else will do. For the persistent seeker, however, home awaits. And not such a home as you had in the childhood of faith, but one full-grown and mature— a blossom, no, a *fruit* called relationship with your Father in heaven.

Surprised by Literalness

It was the early 1970s and the young man, a believer of only six months, sat reading his Bible in the living room of the communal Jesus Freak house in Phoenix. Suddenly, one of the brothers burst through the door. "They found Noah's Ark!" he cried excitedly.

"Yeah," replied the other. "Up on Mount Ararat, right?"

"Right. How did you know? I just barely got the news."

"Says it was parked on Mount Ararat right here in the Bible. I don't need someone to go find it up there to prove it. God said it—that's enough."

♨ ♨ ♨

When people question the literalness of the Bible, archeology often surprises them. And even when archeology disagrees with the Biblical account, the science is usually just a few years from discovering the truth of the Bible record. In either case, the Bible was right all along. Only the world's (and sometimes the church's) opinion vacillated.

For years, archeologists argued against Isaiah 52:4 where the verse plainly says, "My people went down at the first into Egypt to reside there, then the Assyrian oppressed them without cause."

"See, see," they said, "a mistake in the Bible. There were no Assyrians in Egypt at the time." But the taunts ceased a few years later when it was discovered that the Pharaoh of Egypt at the time of the Exodus was an Assyrian who had married into the Egyptian royal family.

Dozens of such discoveries have not slowed the all-out, worldwide search for historical "inaccuracies" in the Bible. Accepting the Bible literally is odious to man. He would then have to acknowledge that God has a *right* to rule men's lives. I sometimes wonder if the Old Testament Jewish scholars questioned the literalness of "Behold, a virgin will be with child and bear a son."[3] Did they think it was merely symbolic? poetic? hyperbolic? But it is certainly far more understandable for them to question *before* the fulfillment than it is for our modern theologians to doubt *after the fact.*

Even the disciples had problems with literalness. Recall their puzzlement when Jesus told them that He must "be put to death" and "rise from the dead." Did they, as many modern believers seem to think, imagine that when He said, "If I be lifted up" that He meant He would be *exalted?*

More often than not, God's Word is literal. But we, the deluded humans, refuse to see it until it actually happens—and sometimes, not *then.* We seem to be ever surprised by God's capacity to tell it like it *will be.* God somehow always turns out to be right. Yet, as often as this happens, we shrink from accepting God's obvious attempt to communicate in plain language.

At one time it was thought that the New Testament was written in some highly specialized Greek especially designed for lofty Christian concepts. And yes, it *was* highly specialized Greek, but designed for daily communication; it was the language of the ordinary people. God was not trying to talk to trained theologians; He was trying to get the gospel to the poor. He *wants* to communicate, not complicate. Certainly, there are deep and esoteric truths in the Bible, but they all rest on simple, clear truth expressed by God in a way that even a child can understand, if we will only believe what He says.

First Things First

If you do not know some phonics, you would not be reading this. To you, it would simply be α κονφυσινγ στρινγ οφ σηαπεσ.[4] The first rule in reading is knowing the sounds associated with the shapes on the page—in other words, phonics.

In law, one must know the origins of law, the case law precedents, and the principle upon which the decision was based.

In every field of endeavor, certain primary knowledge is necessary to accurately understand the whole. In most cases, one must return to the beginnings of a thing to comprehend it. Thus, it is no accident that the Bible's first book is Genesis, which means "beginnings." The beginnings for our faith in Christ are rooted in Genesis, the *least trusted book of the Bible*. But remember that the beginning of that first lie was, "Hath God said . . . ?" In this instance, "Hath God said what is in Genesis?"

However, in their mad dash to publish the gospel of the kingdom, many Christians have failed to attend to these foundations of their faith. Most often, seasoned believers advise new believers to read the New Testament first (I have done it myself). This would be less of a problem in a society of elemental Christian presuppositions such as America was two hundred years ago. Nearly everyone then was familiar with the stories of Genesis and generally accepted the teaching of Creation, the fall of man, and the Deluge. This understanding was a foundation for comprehending the gospel. But today when there is no such consensus and, in fact, rabid disagreement, the gospel has no foundation on which to stand. Even many believers have no firm ground for their beliefs because they refuse to accept the Genesis account. They accept the doctrines of Christianity without knowing why they should. And then often hold beliefs that directly contradict the presuppositions necessary for the gospel.

The real question to today's believer is, "Hath God said, 'In the beginning God created . . .' as He has written? And hath God said that He did it in six days?"

The Genesis-Gospel Connection

> Christianity is—must be—totally committed to the special creation as described in Genesis, and Christianity must fight with all its full might, fair or foul, against the theory of evolution. . . . It becomes clear now that the whole justification of Jesus' life and death is predicated on the existence of Adam and the forbidden fruit he and Eve ate. Without original sin, who needs to be redeemed? Without Adam's fall into a life of constant sin terminated by death, what is the purpose of Christianity? None.[5]

Amen! Preach it, Brother . . . ah . . . Brother . . . ah . . . Falwell? No? Brother Graham? No?

Try "Brother" G. Richard Bozarth writing for *The American Atheist* magazine. Here an atheist has seen what many of America's Bible teachers and preachers have missed—the connection between Genesis and the Gospels. Why, for instance, as this "Biblical expositor" above noted, *would* I need a savior if man never fell? Again, why should we practice monogamous marriage if God didn't create them male and female to become one flesh?

Only "religious experts" question the plain wording in the Genesis story. Nonbelieving language experts all agree that the writer of the words in the Genesis creation account intended them to be believed literally—not allegorically, poetically, figuratively, or symbolically. The nonbelievers may not *believe* Genesis, but they know it was intended to be historical.

Besides, how much sense would the gospel make without the precedent-setting work of Genesis? Consider reading one of the gospels with the following doctrines missing:

- God created everything and He makes the rules.
- God created one man and one woman to be lifetime partners in marriage.
- There was no death before sin.
- Man and nature are fallen because of sin and need saving.
- Man's relationship with God is broken.
- Death is an unnatural state brought about by sin.
- God's justice demands payment for sin.
- God promised a savior who will banish sin and death.
- God created the nation of Israel to bring forth the savior.
- The savior was to come from the tribe of Judah.

And I could go on; this is just a sample. But since many modern Christians have thrown their sextant (an instrument for sighting a star in sea navigation) overboard, the ship has been tossed back and forth by whatever wind that is blowing. Without Genesis (the sextant), it is impossible to properly align to the guiding star. Without it, also, God's Biblical preoccupation with tiny Israel makes Him just another ranting local deity who trashes His people's enemies—sometimes. The promise of the Messiah is gone and the logic of God insisting on Israel remaining separate from the gentile nations disappears. Heterosexual monogamous marriage becomes merely a cultural preference. Is it any wonder that Satan's seven lies work on us? We don't have anything on which to stand!

If we are to avoid the deceptions of Satan, we must return to the Word of God. That return, of necessity, must begin at the beginning—"In the beginning God created." Our main opponent in this return to the beginning is the teaching called evolution. Though ancient evolution came packaged as pagan religions, modern evolution is under a guise of science. Pagan creation myths almost exclusively began, like modern theories, with *spontaneous generation of life*—usually the life of the gods, but there was no original Creator. In ancient and modern evolution, the authorship of God and His establishment of moral standards are eliminated.

I can say with certainty that the modern theory of evolution is not science in the sense of a systematic search for truth; there is *no* proof for evolution. Even world-class scientists are beginning to admit this. After studying evolution for over forty years, Professor N. Heribert-Nilsson of Lund University in Sweden said that the deficiencies of the transitional forms in the fossil record "are real, they will never be filled." He wrote a little parody: Faith is the substance of fossils hoped for, the evidence of links unseen.[6]

However, I am not going to attempt to make an evidentiary case for creation and against evolution in these pages. People such as Dr. Henry Morris, Ken Ham, and others at the Institute for Creation Research (ICR) are much more qualified to do so. They have stood for years against the raging, howling ridicule of both atheists and "reasonable" preachers for their beliefs. Don't just believe me when I say the evidence of both science and history all confirms the Genesis account; read the evidence for yourself.[7]

With evolution, it matters not whether one is an atheist or believer, whether one believes in gradual or sudden evolution, or if one tosses God into the mix, such as with theistic evolution, day/age theories, guided evolution, or bizarre "gap" theories. All of these theories deny basic tenets of the Word that are necessary for the gospel of Christ to have meaning.

The Bible says:	The Evolutionist says:
Man is created by God and in God's image. Man is higher than the animals.	Man is an animal and from the animals.
Adam and Eve were the first humans. All others are descended from them.	Man-like creatures evolved in different places and different times.
The heavens and the earth and all that is in them were created by God in six calendar days.	Everything came accidentally from nothing, by no one, over billions of years.
Both man and animals were created to reproduce "each after their own kind."	Animals may adapt to become other species over time.
There was no death before Adam's sin. Death came to the world through sin.	Struggle and death are the means of growth and improvement of the species.
Marriage was established by God.	Marriage was purely a survival mechanism for primitive societies.
Man was created innocent but is now corrupt because of Adam's fall. All men have the fallen nature. Man is basically evil.	Man was created by his environment. As the fittest survive, man improves. Man is neutral or basically good.
Man needs to be changed internally by God.	Man can be improved by proper heredity and environment.
Good and evil are fixed by God.	Good and evil adapt to the changing world.
God destroyed the earth by worldwide flood.	The earth was formed either gradually or through a series of smaller cataclysms.

This does not exhaust the list. For instance, Israel makes its first appearance early in Genesis. Also, the explanation of man's languages is there. But even this partial list shows clearly that it would be impossible to believe some of the most essential doctrines of Christianity and still cling to evolution. Nor could we trust the founder of Christianity much because He (Jesus) treated the Genesis accounts as factual. What greater authority could you ask for? In fact, all New Testament treatments of Genesis stories presume them to be historical as opposed to symbolic or poetic. Perhaps, if we cannot trust Genesis, we cannot trust any of the Bible writers who were foolish enough to believe in a literal creation and flood. And, as I have said before, if the first five words (or any words, for that matter) of the Bible are untrue, none of it can be trusted.

If we are to return to the solid foundation of God's Word and escape the lies that bind, we will have to reconcile ourselves to the truth of Genesis. We must choose to believe the Bible.

Choose This Day . . .

"How long will you hesitate between two opinions?" asked Elijah. "If the LORD is God, follow Him; but if Baal, follow him."[8] This is the daily challenge to the believer. When we become aware of what is God's will, we must choose—between life and death, and between blessing and cursing (see Deuteronomy 30:19–20).

Our compromise and capitulation to the lies of Satan have not only bound us but have tarred the name of God with the resulting mire. The name of Christ is blasphemed because of our willful confusion. If we have chosen to believe lies out of ignorance, let us now acknowledge our sin and turn to our gracious Father. If we have hardened our necks in rebellion, let us bow the knee and seek His mercy. He will restore us and, in doing so, will restore our witness before the world as those who represent the great and glorious God.

But turn to Him we must.

"If we confess our sins, He is faithful and righteous to forgive us our sins and to cleanse us from all unrighteousness," He says in 1 John 1:9. The only safety from the lies that bind is a tenacious clinging to truth. God has said His Word is truth, will we believe it? His promise is more than forgiveness—it is restoration. If we return to His care, He will cleanse us from all unrighteousness.

The opportunity still exists for us to retrieve our navigational tools and focus on our Star. The question is, do we have the courage to admit our foolishness and the humility to put the sextant back to our eye?

Review

This chapter may be summarized in the following points:

- The American church is adrift because it has abandoned Biblical truth.

- The return to stability begins with admitting our need and a return to Biblical inerrancy.

- The study of Genesis is essential to proper doctrine.

- The church must chose between believing God's Word and charting its own course.

ELEVEN

EYES ON THE PRIZE

I f you are still reading at this point, it is possible that you are ready to take action against the lies that bind you and your culture. Jesus commanded His disciples to be salt and light in this world, but many of us have hidden ourselves away in the salt shaker or, perhaps grown utterly tasteless. But Hebrews is very instructive. We must return to "the elementary principles" of the Word of God. There is no other option.

> For though by this time you ought to be teachers, you have need again for someone to teach you the elementary principles of the oracles [words] of God, and you have come to need milk and not solid food. For every one who partakes only of milk is not accustomed to the word of righteousness, for he is a babe. But solid food is . for the mature, who because of practice have their senses trained to discern good and evil. (Hebrews 5:12–14)

Assuming that we turn away from our lackadaisical treatment of God's Word and ask God's mercy in being delivered from the confines of deception, we must then turn to making the *choice* to believe the Scriptures. When I was a new Christian, I was taught that it was *my* responsibility to know and understand my Lord and His will. This is not to say that it was my human efforts that produced this knowledge, but my decision to become intimately familiar with His Word allowed the Holy Spirit to illumine my mind. My "method," as it were, was to read the text, look up cross-references, look up verses with the same words and topics, and pray that God would open my eyes to what *He* wanted to say.

I must confess that this has not always been my practice. I, like any other person, have carnal motives that try to disguise themselves as proper intentions. These will sometimes distort my conclusions. But God is light and I regularly pray for Him to expose these self-delusions. On one occasion, I recall having a long-standing question of doctrine before the Lord. After several years, I became impatient and struck out on my own to find the answer—and I found one! Let me tell you, it was the most convoluted and ridiculous eschatological hypothesis I have ever heard (and I have heard some of the weirdest). By God's grace and my youthful enthusiasm over my newfound discovery, I went immediately to my pastor to share it. But when I arrived, the pastor was deeply embroiled in a discussion of Scripture (on a totally unrelated subject) with his mother. As I listened, the pastor cited verses to support his contention—verses which, bit by bit, demolished my precious new doctrine. When the conversation was finished, the pastor turned and asked, "Now, what was it you wanted to share with me?" "Never mind," I said, and I walked home repenting and rejoicing. Repenting for trying to force God to reveal His Word on my timetable and rejoicing that His grace had spared me a long-term, destructive delusion. Only after this did I finally receive the answer I was waiting for.

When we begin studying the Bible, the list in Hebrews 6:1–2 is helpful.

> Therefore leaving the elementary teaching about the Christ, let us press on to maturity, not laying again a foundation of repentance from dead works and of faith toward God, of instruction about washings, and laying on of hands, and the resurrection of the dead, and eternal judgment.

Early in my education in the Scriptures, I was given the task of producing a solid Bible study on each of these topics. That foundation has held me in good stead. Again, I remind you of the importance of Genesis when you are studying.

It is not always easy to believe the Bible, especially when believing it means you are wrong about something. Often it seems we are alone in believing the literal words of Scripture. The whole world is constantly in opposition to God's Word—it is the world's very nature. When I said earlier that the flesh is probably our worst enemy, this was not to suggest that the world and the devil are absent from the scene. Between the two, they conspire to rob us of our faith by means of every media from billboards to satellite broadcast television. Not only is the message itself corrupt and anti-Christian, but the very *medium* of television is designed for a-musement (a= not, and muse= to think, i.e., not to think). We are being trained by the media to be entertained *without thinking*. Our attention spans are shortened because of the staccato-cut sequences of most TV fare. It is small wonder that Christians begin looking at their watches about fifteen minutes into a sermon. Even "good" television is deceptive about its import. Neil Postman in his eloquent and incisive book, *Amusing Ourselves to Death* (Penguin, 1985), wryly noted, "Therein is our problem, for television is at its most trivial and, therefore, most dangerous when its aspirations are high, when it presents itself as a carrier of important cultural conversations."

I am *not* saying that television of itself is evil. This would be the same error as lumping all rock music (lipstick, dancing, etc.) under the title of evil. It is TV's *uses* I am addressing.

It is even more foolish, then, to bombard ourselves with "Christian" books and television shows that patently undercut the inerrancy of the Bible (unless you are reading "enemy" literature for the purposes of refuting it). Yet, we buy and read books from our local Christian bookseller by authors who have nothing better to do than to spread their personal doubts to a large and gullible audience. Then, backed by their Ph.D's, they proceed to tell us that doubting is good for us. No doctrine escapes such unbelief-in-print. I am reminded of some of the current teachings by Robert Schuller, that man was *worthy* of Christ's death on the cross. Such a teaching renders the sacrificial love of Christ as a mere *even trade* for our souls. Implicit is unbelief regarding man's sinfulness. It might do these writers (and their readers) some good to consider the implications of Revelations 21:8 where the "unbelieving" are second on the list of those whose "part will be in the lake that burns with fire and brimstone."

After we commit to believing God, as we come to know God in prayer and His Word, we become more and more familiar with *how He thinks*. I may sound as though I am promoting some sort of extrabiblical knowledge, but I am not. I am saying that as we delve into the Word, the Word by the Spirit delves into us in a way that is beyond our conscious knowledge of teachings and verses. Because our interaction with the Word is a part of a friendship with God (see John 15:15), He begins to rub off on us. This sometimes leads to an uncanny ability to "know" that something is wrong or right before one can put a finger on the exact Biblical principle.

Immersion in the Word is primary to this, and we are exhorted to lend ourselves to prayer, reading, and study to facilitate the Holy Spirit's work "until Christ is formed in you" (see Galatians 4:19). Does this sound like voluntary brainwashing? You bet it is! Our brains *need* washing as much as our souls. In either event, the entire world system is already brainwashing you whether you realize it or not. In truth, most Christians today are scarcely able to discern the powerful forces that seek to warp their thinking and which are causing many of the problems of the church today. But twentieth-century believers have lost something—they have lost any understanding of *why they believe* what they believe. They no longer are trained in *apologetics*—the ability to argue the position of their faith. In fact, we have almost altogether lost the ability to think critically. Yet, in 1 Peter 3:15 we read, "Sanctify Christ as Lord in your hearts [acknowledge He is always right], always being ready to make a defense to every one who asks you to give an account of the hope that is in you."

How would someone give an account of his hope that he will "lay aside the old self with its evil practices" if man had evolved (and thus not fallen) or was basically good? If man is not fallen, there is no hope of recovery from a fall—it never happened!

We must *exercise* ourselves unto godliness—the godliness of believing God's Word—by learning the *why* of our faith. Christians in the past believed such an ability was a given; we should strive to make intelligent Christianity once again the norm. This does not insure that nonbelievers will no longer think of us as a bunch of bumpkins, but it may insure that the accusation is not true.

There has not been a lot of critical evaluation of issues from an inerrant Bible perspective in modern times. Because of this lack, we must relearn the capacities of critical thinking. After we begin to familiarize ourselves with the Bible we should begin to read works of apologetics—what I call, literature of literalness—and see how other believers are defending their hope. Not only can we learn to explain and defend our faith, we will be encouraged to read of others who believe the Bible literally.

Naturally, we do not want to fall into the trap of trying to *prove the Bible* by science or reason, since the Bible has God's own assurance of truth. We are seeking examples or illustrations of how the world really is what the Bible says it is. For instance, in the late Middle Ages "science" said the earth was flat, but the Bible has always described the earth as a sphere (see Isaiah 40:22). Many church leaders of that time conformed their theology to this assertion of "science," and the church has paid dearly for the error. God's Word proves the world's truth, not the other way around.

The Literature of Literalness

Allow me to suggest some books that will help you in this way. I do not intend to make an exhaustive list here, but these will provide a beginning. And speaking of beginnings, I will first recommend books on the truth of Genesis. Remember, even with these books it is *your* responsibility to check their teachings against God's Word.

- *The Genesis Record,* by Dr. Henry M. Morris (Baker Book House, Grand Rapids, MI, 1989) bills itself as a "scientific and devotional commentary on the book of beginnings." It takes the reader through the book of

Genesis nearly verse by verse, giving a believing scientist's look at God's record of the Creation, Flood, Israel, and other important topics. This is not a quick read, but Morris's deliberate and thorough style leaves little unanswered and much explained.

- *The Lie,* by Ken Ham (Master Books, El Cajon, CA, 1987) is an overview of how the evolutionary lie undercuts all primary Christian doctrine. Ham's writing is witty and readable—and right! A good one to break in the Creation argument.

- *Pilgrim's Progress,* by John Bunyan (many editions and publishers) is a fiction written in a time (1600s) when apologetics was standard training for real believers. The story has many apologetical sections woven throughout in an objection/ answer format which was common at the time. Basic Christian doctrines are eloquently, systematically, and thoroughly defended. A Christian classic that no believer should miss. I read it at least once every five years and am always surprised at what I missed last time.

- *The Holy War,* by John Bunyan again. This is a more difficult fiction but contains many more objection/answer defenses of the faith. Being a child of the television era, I find it hard to follow the answers all the way from "Firstly" to "Twenty-seventhly" but it is worth the mental discipline to do it.

- *Evidence That Demands a Verdict, volumes I and II,* by Josh McDowell (Here's Life Publishers, San Bernadino, CA, 1972 & 1979) is all you ever wanted to know about the Bible and why it is all true. These volumes, billed as "historical evidences for the Christian faith," examine the trustworthiness of Scripture, the existence of Jesus, the Resurrection, messianic prophecies, and much more. Arranged in a handy outline format.

- *Revealing the New Age Jesus* by Douglas Groothuis (Inter-Varsity Press, Downers Grove, IL, 1990) is an excellent apologetic comparing the Biblical Jesus with the pale and wan "New Age" avatar and all-around sweetie presented by the neopagans. Devastating to the mystical view of our Savior.

- *Why I Believe*, by Dr. D. James Kennedy (Word Books, Waco, TX, 1980) takes individual topics such as Biblical inerrancy, God, Creation, heaven, hell, and others individually and gives a brief explanation of why he believes in each. Kennedy shows that both observable science and reason illustrate scriptural doctrines.

- *The Great Evangelical Disaster*, by Francis A. Schaeffer (Crossway Books, Westchester, IL, 1984) was his parting shot—a last warning about the flickering candle of Christian civilization in the West. The key to revival: Believe the Bible! Schaeffer makes a powerful case from history and present conditions to show the dire state of affairs in America and the road back, if we will choose to take it.

- *A Full Quiver*, by Rick and Jan Hess (Wolgemuth and Hyatt, Brentwood, TN, 1990) looks at the long-standing, and recently discarded, Biblical doctrine opposing birth control. This unpopular position is ably argued by the Hesses through Scripture. Probably their most important verses are taken from Genesis.

- *The Bible and Birth Control*, by Charles D. Provan (Zimmer Printing, 410 West Main Street, Monongahela, PA, 15063, 1989) is a concise presentation of the church's consistent opposition to birth control. Provan demonstrates that this was not some kind of "Catholic thing" by quoting such notables as Luther, Calvin, Wesley, and other Protestants in their uniform condemnation of the practice. Both this and the Hess's book are prime examples of how to defend an unpopular belief even within the church.

Lights!

"While you're going past the switch, would you turn on the dark, honey?"

It sounds odd, doesn't it? You can't turn on the dark. You can, however turn on a light that will send the dark scurrying under and behind anything it can. When you do turn on the light, whatever is happening in the dark is suddenly exposed. As Ephesians 5:13 says, "All things become visible when they are exposed by the light, for everything that becomes visible is light."

Lies are psychic darkness. No lie is successful in the glare of truth. No one can "turn on" a lie where there is light. Having our own lights on means being sure of God's Word. But there is still plenty of darkness around, and for that we need a different tactic—exposure! "Do not participate in the unfruitful deeds of darkness," Ephesians 5:11 says, "but instead even expose them."

This is the other half of apologetics—exposing untrue beliefs as darkness and lies. We are called to be salt and light in the world; therefore, we must begin to examine all new teachings against the Word of God. Many writers have blazed a trail in exposing many of the lies mentioned in this book.

- *The Collapse of Creation,* by Scott M. Huse (Baker Book House, Grand Rapids, MI, 1983) dismantles the dogma of evolution from the standpoint of Scripture as well as numerous scientific disciplines. He cites specific natural phenomena that could not have evolved and quotes evolutionary scientists who realize the impossibility of their beliefs.

- *The Seduction of Christianity,* by Dave Hunt and T. A. McMahon (Harvest House, Eugene, OR, 1985) is fast becoming a classic of scriptural exposure of the lies of

New Age doctrine and practices. This is not merely "hype" but a careful look at the failure of Christianity to meet the challenge of paganism.

- *The Way Home,* by Mary Pride (Crossway Books, Westchester, IL, 1985) absolutely demolishes the feminist influence in the church. This will expose ideas that you would not have otherwise known which had their roots in what Mary calls "humanism on the half-shell." Very challenging—*don't* miss this one.

- *The Danger of Self-Love,* by Paul Brownback (Moody Press, Chicago, IL, 1982) is as straight as its title. Tightly organized arguments from Scripture expose the whole self-esteem movement as old-fashioned pride. However, it does not allow you to set up the false dichotomy of having high or low self-esteem, but rather presents the Bible's solution.

- *Psychoheresy,* by Martin and Deidre Bobgan (East Gate Publishers, Santa Barbara, CA, 1987) does to the whole field of psychology what Brownback does to self-esteem. It includes even the evidence of psychological tests that show psychoanalysis to be ineffective at best, and dangerous at worst.

- *Bad News for Modern Man,* by Frankie Schaeffer (Crossway Books, Westchester, IL, 1984) is an acid bath for American culture, both sacred and secular. Strong medicine!

- *Whatever Happened to the Human Race?,* by Francis A. Schaeffer and C. Everett Koop, M.D. (Fleming H. Revell, Old Tappan, NJ, 1979) is a reasoned, scriptural look at overall Western society's decline and how it may be reversed.

- *Ancient Empires of the New Age,* by Paul deParrie and Mary Pride (Crossway Books, Westchester IL, 1989) exposes the ancient pagan origins of New Age doctrines and practices.

- *Romanced to Death,* by Paul deParrie (Wolgemuth and Hyatt, Brentwood, TN, 1990) shows the origins of the sexual revolution in the abandonment of the Biblical purpose of marriage and sex, and Western culture's dangerous flirtation with antibiblical definitions of love.

Action!

You are in the greatest danger of all when you study and believe God's Word. Now that you can defend the truth and expose the darkness, you face the possibility of your greatest failure—or most exciting challenge.

Faith without works is dead, not to mention deadly. God saves us with *purpose.* He reveals His Word by the Holy Spirit for more than our personal security and faith. He has a plan, and we are part of it. We are called to be laborers in the kingdom. As Joab encouraged Israel, "Be strong and let us show ourselves courageous for the sake of our people and for the cities of our God; and may the LORD do what is good in His sight" (2 Samuel 10:12).

Jesus told us that those who hear the Word and do not do it have built their houses on sand—that all of their cherished structures have no real security unless they are existing in the real world, as God defines *real.* What good would it be to quote Scripture on feeding the hungry to a starving man? It would be sheer hypocrisy!

So after all the work of seeking the truth in God's Word and escaping the lies of Satan, don't deceive yourself that you may simply absorb all that knowledge without having to go out into the world with it. Christ has called us to *action*—to war! Christianity is not safe! Today's "churchianity" is safe precisely to the degree that it is *not* Christian. We are commanded to "occupy until He comes." We are warned that we will be sent like sheep among wolves and that *all* who live godly lives will suffer persecution. The reason most Christians in America have never suffered any real persecution is because they never *do* their Christianity!

If you hide your lamp under a bushel, then it will not send light out that exposes darkness. The only time those in darkness try to terrorize believers is when the believers expose evil deeds and begin to serve the victims of the wicked. All of Christian history bears this out, even when the wicked who were being exposed were the church leaders (perhaps, *especially* then).

Christians think they are supposed to be *nice*, but niceness is not a fruit of the Spirit—gentleness and meekness, yes, but not niceness or politeness or pusillanimity. Church people are often mortally offended when other believers are bold to expose evil. How would they have felt about that raving lunatic John the Baptist? And Paul the apostle was not very polite either. Even Jesus—Jesus was simply *not nice.* For two thousand years, the believers have run to the cutting edge, pushing their culture and society toward unheard-of moral commitments.

"Stop infanticide! Stop slavery! Stop adultery!" the believers cried—and always at the most inconvenient times! All this at times when the "slow, tactful way" was vaunted as the way to go. But, no. These nuts had to go out and get arrested, jailed, killed, and worse, *sued* for their godly obedience. This is the true history of Christian service!

But it is not this history we hear about—the thousands of missionaries dead in unknown graves. When we hear the tales of the great men—Knox, Luther, Fox, Wycliffe—they are all safely and sleepily tucked away in the past "when real reforms were needed." That is not like *today,* we are told. All the important battles are done and there is no longer a need for radicals like Bunyan to rain fiery words of doom on the corrupt church of his time; no more need for men like William Booth to walk the midnight streets of the London slums to rescue ragged prostitutes and drunks from their animalistic lives; no more need for people like the early Roman Christians to risk their lives and break the law to save the infants that the Roman rich exposed for death because of a flawed ear or nose; no more need for women like Corrie Ten Boom to risk all to hide a few destitute Jews.

I speak foolishly. Of course, those issues exist today. And it is still the job of believers to *act* even at the risk of personal security and comfort. After all, what do you think all these I mentioned have risked? Risking death, imprisonment, torture, loss of property, loss of livelihood, loss of community respect, did these believers excuse themselves because their actions would have an adverse effect *on their families?* No! They knew that the worst effect on their children would occur if they *failed* to stand for truth. Most Christians today do not understand that believers in the past were almost *never* arrested for being Christians. Check for yourself; look up the records. Every one was charged and convicted of a *legitimate crime.* In Rome, they were killed for disturbing the peace or sedition or treason. Rev. Richard Wurmbrand, author of *Tortured for Christ* (Bantam Books, 1977), spent fourteen years in a Rumanian Communist torture chamber for contempt of court. He would not surrender a list of those to whom he ministered. In 1984, Pastor Everett Sileven in Nebraska, along with several men in his congregation were jailed for contempt of court when they refused to quit teaching their children in their church school. Today, hundreds are being sued and jailed for disturbing the peace outside abortion clinics, for trespassing to save babies from death, and jailed indefinitely for contempt of court when they refuse to promise that they will not obey God in rescuing babies.

No, Christianity is not safe! But we must learn to fight in God's way and on God's issues. Most Christians need to be convinced that this comfortable Christianity they are experiencing is *not* true Christianity. They need to be convinced that Scripture demands that *they* act at all, then *how* they should act.

The first books will deal with the fact that Christians *must act*, then there are books that give some courses of action on a number of issues.

- *Foxe's Book of Martyrs*, by John Foxe (many publishers) is a sampling of what real Christians have done with their faith for the last 2,000 years, and what they have *paid* to do it.

- *The Cost of Discipleship*, by Deitrich Bonhoeffer (Macmillan, New York, NY, 1963) who was a modern martyr killed by the Nazi regime. He offers a powerful argument from Scripture on our responsibility to obey God at all costs. Dangerous to the flesh!

- *Life Together*, by Deitrich Bonhoeffer (Harper and Row, New York, NY, 1954) will challenge some of your most comfortable assumptions about church life. "It is not to be taken for granted that the Christian has the privilege of living among other Christians," he begins on the first page. *Heresy*, we think, but Bonhoeffer blows the accusation away.

- *A Christian Manifesto*, by Francis A. Schaeffer (Crossway Books, Westchester, IL, 1981) is just what it bills itself to be—a manifesto of Christianity acting Christian.

- *Competent to Counsel*, by Jay E. Adams (Zondervan, Grand Rapids, MI, 1970) is an excellent training tool in *Biblical*, as opposed to humanistic, counseling. Adams does not just dismantle the pagan counseling, he gives concrete instruction in how Christians should counsel. Many have denigrated Adams's "nouthetic" method as "turn-or-burn" counseling. The question here is, "If they *don't* turn, won't they burn?" Other books by Adams are also recommended.

- *A Time for Anger,* by Frankie Schaeffer (Crossway Books, Westchester, IL, 1982) is a declaration of war for modern Christians who have finally awakened to the fact that the secular world is *not* neutral and has, in fact, already declared war on Christianity.

- *Closed: 99 Ways to Stop Abortion,* by Joseph Scheidler (Crossway Books, Westchester, IL, 1985) briefly outlines each of 99 tactics that will save babies. Some are political, others are more direct ways.

- *Is Rescuing Right?,* by Randy Alcorn (Inter-Varsity Press, Downers Grove, IL, 1990) is an excellent defense of abortion clinic rescues (blocking doors) from the points of Scripture and church history.

- *The Rescuers,* by Paul deParrie (Wolgemuth and Hyatt, Brentwood, TN, 1989) is the stories of ordinary Christians who risk their reputations and their freedom to save babies from death. What kind of nuts do this? Read it and find out.

- *All the Way Home,* by Mary Pride (Crossway Books, Westchester, IL, 1989) is the practical outworking of her book *The Way Home* which I listed under "Literature of Exposure." A *must read* book.

- *With Justice for All,* by John Perkins (Regal Books, Ventura, CA, 1982) describes a Christian response to poverty. This is no mere theory but practical work as lived by the author.

As I have said, this is only a beginner's list, but it is a place to start. Jesus commissioned His disciples to disciple the world, and we must either take up that commission or fade from His kingdom. Now is the time to turn to Him and take up the challenge:

> Go therefore *and make disciples of all nations,* baptizing them in the name of the Father and the Son and the Holy Spirit, teaching them to observe all that I commanded you; and lo, I am with you always, even to the end of the age. (Matthew 28:19–20, emphasis added)

Review

This chapter may be summarized by the following points:

- Repent of unbelief.
- Chose to believe the Bible.
- Learn the truth.
- Learn to defend the truth.
- Turn on the light—expose the evil works of darkness.
- Do the Word of God.

NOTES

Chapter One: In the Beginning Was the Lie

1. Romans 1:13; 11:25; 1 Corinthians 10:1; 12:1; 2 Corinthians 1:8; 1 Thessalonians 4:13.

2. 2 Corinthians 2:11, KJV.

3. 1 Corinthians 14:20; Ephesians 5:12; Philippians 4:8.

Chapter Two: Just One Question, Eve

1. A "channeled" spirit being who speaks through the modern necromancer, J. Z. Knight.

2. This was a loan made *with interest* to the man that God had given them as a pastor. The loan itself was deplorable, but the addition of interest was simply wickedness. Yet, this is another discussion for another time.

3. Luke 24:25–26, emphasis added.

4. See Luke 22:49–50; Matthew 16:21–23.

5. *The Oregonian*, 12 November 1988.

6. Isaiah 45:9.

7. I mentioned a specific experience of this kind of teaching in my book, *Romanced to Death* (Wolgemuth & Hyatt, 1990) on pages 188–190.

8. During the late 1960s I read a "street language" paraphrase of the New Testament. This dubious work translated Paul's advice in 1 Corinthians 7:36 about how a man deals with his virgin daughter to saying that if a man was having sex with his "old lady" (girlfriend), they were not sinning so long as they were going to

get married. This idea is not limited to hippies, however. I have come across many believers, including clergy, who justify fornication in this way.

9. 1 Corinthians 6:1–8.

10. There is no book of Hezekiah. This mythical book is where many believers place "verses" that people believe are Biblical but are not.

11. Sara Rubenstein, "Evangelicals Urge an End to Violence," *The Oregonian*, 3 March 1987, and personal communications.

12. Luke 15:8–10.

13. Francis Schaeffer, *The Great Evangelical Disaster* (Westchester, IL: Crossway Books, 1984), 43–44.

14. Institute for Creation Research (ICR), P.O. Box 266, El Cajon, CA 92021, (619) 448–1121, is a valuable resource for those who believe the Bible's historical account of the creation (minus all the "gap" theories and other subterfuges).

15. Genesis 3:12–13 (deParrie Paraphrase, All Rights Reversed).

16. Numbers 22.

17. John 16:13–15.

Chapter Three: The Altered Word

1. Margie Boule, "Obscenity in Eye of Beholder," *The Oregonian*, 8 May 1990.

2. John 10:10.

3. Matthew 18:15–17.

4. Romans 14.

5. Mark 7:8–9.

6. To those who propose the vegetarian spirituality/carnivorous carnality doctrine, I derive some pleasure in pointing out that Adolf Hitler was a vegetarian and Francis of Assisi carnivorous.

7. Mark 7:18–19.

8. Romans 14:6.

Chapter Four: The Dissolution of Death and Judgment

1. *The Skeptical Feminist*, Barbara G. Walker (San Francisco: Harper and Row, 1987), 58.

2. Joanna Cherry, "On Consideration of Not Dying," *The New Times*, vol. 4, no. 2 (July 1988):12.

3. Joe Fisher, *The Case for Reincarnation*, as quoted in *The New Age Catalogue* (Island Publications, 1988), 106.

4. *The New Age Catalogue*, 102.

5. The Grail was reputed to give immortality to the one who drank from it.

6. Matthew 6:27, KJV.

7. In an interview in *Magical Blend* magazine (issue 13, 1986): 23. Quoted by Texe Marrs in *Dark Secrets of the New Age* (Westchester IL: Crossway Books, 1987), 142.

8. This has been particularly true among Socialists and Marxists. None of these, however, has offered any explanation of how such a system came into being in a materialistic universe, nor how concepts of "right" or "wrong" fit into this system.

9. I heard this particular breakdown preached at my church by Chris Stewart in July of 1990. I am indebted to him for this simple and accurate assessment of sin's effect.

10. 2 Samuel 12:1–15. Nathan completes this statement by saying "you shall not die." This is in no sense the same as the Serpent's version of that line. Nathan was simply telling David that he was not to undergo the death penalty, which was the penalty for both adultery and murder.

11. Isaiah 45:9.

12. Isaiah 45:24.

13. Proverbs 9:10.

14. Psalms 37:1–2.

15. John Dart, "Pastors Need Humility, Schuller Advises," *Los Angeles Times*, 18 January 1986.

Chapter Five: Sold by Suggestion

1. Genesis 3:1.

2. Deuteronomy 29:29; Matthew 7:7; Hebrews 11:6.

3. Edgar C. Whisenant, World Bible Society, 467 Chestnut St., Nashville, TN 37203 (1988).

4. Edgar C. Whisenant, *The Final Shout: Rapture 1989 Report* (Nashville, TN: World Bible Society, 1989).

5. Quote from *God and the Astronomers* in *Time,* 5 February 1979, 149–150. *Time* essay: "In the Beginning: God and Science," Lance Morrow.

6. Psychology is not a science. A science must have testable, repeatable, and falsifiable theories. The human mind is too individual to have them all tied down to any particular responses.

Chapter Six: The Egoism of Enlightenment

1. *The New Age Catalogue,* 1988.

2. *The New Times,* Seattle, Washington, vol. 4, no. 3, p. 8.

3. (New York: Macmillan Publishing, 1965), 354.

4. *Psychological Seduction* (Nashville: Thomas Nelson, 1983), 16.

5. Ibid, 19–20.

6. "Marketing Techniques Aid Church's Growth," *The Oregonian,* 18 December 1978.

7. "Gallup Poll Indicates Church Reviving," *Christian Update,* May 1984.

8. George W. Cornell, "Pollster Gallup Finds Religion on Rise, Morality Declining," *The Oregonian,* 14 July 1984.

9. A Johns Hopkins study by Zelnik and Kantner reported in Family Planning Perspectives (PP's publication) shows that between 1971 and 1976, sexual activity among these teens increased 41 percent, premarital pregnancy 45 percent, and abortion 100 percent. Information printed in an Intercessors for America publication, *The Monstrosity of Planned Parenthood,* by Gary Bergel.

Chapter Seven: Garden Gods

1. "New Age Harmonies," *Time,* 7 December 1987.

2. Sura Rubenstein, "Shirley MacLaine Helps Others Search for 'Higher Self,' " *The Oregonian,* 30 March 1987.

3. Original source unknown.

4. Quoted in *The Collapse of Evolution* by Scott M. Huse (Grand Rapids, MI: Baker Book House, 1983, reprint 1986), 3.

5. John 10:35.

6. Luke 17:21, KJV.

7. *Humanist Manifesto I* (1933).

8. *Humanist Manifesto II* (1973).

9. Proverbs 16:25.

10. Isaiah 45:5.

11. Numbers 23:19. See also 1 Samuel 15:29.

12. Revelation 7:12, emphasis added.

13. Matthew 28:18, KJV.

14. James 1:17.

15. Exodus 20:11, emphasis added.

16. Job 38:4, 12.

17. Matthew 6:27, KJV.

18. Robert Schuller, *Self-Esteem: The New Reformation,* (p. 68). Quoted in *Moody Monthly,* May 1983.

19. Abraham Maslow, a pagan psychologist and early promoter of the self-esteem teaching, later concurred with this. His research showed that those who had the greatest self-esteem were least likely to help those less fortunate and most likely to oppress those weaker than themselves.

20. *Self-Esteem: The New Reformation,* (p. 19). Quoted in *Moody Monthly,* May 1983.

21. 1 Peter 5:5.

22. *Self-Esteem: The New Reformation,* (p. 75). Quoted in *Moody Monthly,* May 1983.

23. Proverbs 16:18.

24. James Dobson, *Hide or Seek* (Old Tappan, NJ: Revell, 1974), 12–13. Quoted in Paul Brownback, *The Danger of Self-Love* (Chicago, IL: Moody Press, 1982), 15. I highly recommend Brownback's book to those on both sides of the self-esteem issue in the church. This is the clearest *Biblical* exposition of the topic I have seen.

25. *The Danger of Self-Love* (Chicago, IL: Moody Press, 1982), 12.

26. *Self-Esteem: The New Reformation,* (pp. 26–27). Quoted in *Moody Monthly,* May 1983.

27. "When the Clay Molds the Potter," *Moody Monthly,* May 1983, 79.

Chapter Eight: The Abolition of Good and Evil

1. *Beyond Good and Evil* (1886) quoted in *Cortez and the Downfall of the Aztec Empire,* Jon Manchip White (New York:St. Martin's Press, 1971), 63.

2. *Ecstasy Is a New Frequency* (Santa Fe, MN:Bear and Company, 1987), 55.

3. Sura Rubenstein, "Shirley MacLaine Helps Others Search for 'Higher Self,' " *The Oregonian,* 30 March 1987.

4. Isaiah 5:20–21.

5. Richard Cavendish, ed., *Encyclopedia of the Unexplained* New York: McGraw-Hill, 1974), 242–243.

6. Dr. Seymore Feshback first developed the catharsis theory regarding TV violence back in the 1950s. He proposed that TV violence acted as a safety valve for pent-up violence and released it harmlessly before it exploded into actual violent episodes. The theory had the ring of truth and was instantly picked up by pro-pornography groups and psychologists. Feshback, however, continued his research and later discovered that the theory was not only false, but dangerous. The doctor bravely withdrew his original theory to the hoots and jeers of many social scientists.

7. I take this from the few honest reviewers to have seen the movie. Most were too cowed by the "arts" community to be honest about the ponderous script. Some movie reviewers privately admitted that it was a lousy film but that they did not want to be lumped in with fundamentalists if they gave the film its just desserts.

8. I was informed by a professor of psychology that there are really only two psychological schools: (1) Live with your guilt, and (2) Blame someone else. Those I am now discussing are of the latter school.

9. John W. Whitehead, *The Second American Revolution* (Westchester, IL: Crossway Books, 1982), 51, quoting "Natural Law," *Harvard Law Review* vol. 32, 40 and a letter from Mr. Holmes to John C. H. Wu, August 26, 1926. (See Whitehead footnotes on p. 217).

10. Arlie J. Hoover, "Immorality of Plurality Danger in U.S.," *The Oregonian,* 11 November 1978.

11. S. Angus, *The Mystery-Religions* (New York: Dover Publications, 1975), 277–278, 281.

Chapter Nine: The Why of the Lie

1. *The Pride O' Scotland* (Peterhead, Scotland, AB4 7DQ: New Hope Publishers, 1982).

2. Genesis 3:6.

3. This subject is fully dealt with in my book, *Romanced to Death* (Brentwood, TN: Wolgemuth & Hyatt, 1990).

4. See Romans 5:12, 19; 2 Corinthians 11:3; 1 Timothy 2:14.

5. Isaiah 5:13–14.

6. Proverbs 6:23.

Chapter Ten: A Star to Steer Her By

1. Paul deParrie, *The Rescuers* (Brentwood, TN: Wolgemuth & Hyatt, 1989), 124.

2. Revelation 2:4–5.

3. Isaiah 7:14, NAS.

4. Pronounced phonetically, this nonsense group of Greek words would say, "a confusing string of shapes."

5. September 1978, 19. Quoted in *The Lie*, Ken Ham (El Cajon, CA: Master Books, 1987), 74.

6. Both of these quotes were found and have sources noted in *The Collapse of Evolution*, Scott M. Huse (Grand Rapids, MI: Baker Book House, 1983), 42–43.

7. Institute for Creation Research, P.O. Box 2667, El Cajon, CA 92021 (619) 448–1121.

8. 1 Kings 18:21.

INDEX

ABOUT THE AUTHOR

P aul deParrie is a Christian activist and social commentator. He is editor of *The Advocate* magazine and author of a number of books including *Romanced to Death* (Wolgemuth & Hyatt), *The Rescuers* (Wolgemuth & Hyatt), and *Unholy Sacrifices of the New Age* (Crossway).

Paul has six children, one grandchild, and lives with his wife in Portland, Oregon.

The typeface for the text of this book is *Palatino*. This type—best known as a contemporary *italic* typeface—was a post-World War II design crafted by the talented young German calligrapher Hermann Zapf. For inspiration, Zapf drew upon the writing legacy of a group of Italian Renaissance writing masters, in which the typeface's namesake, Giovanni Battista Palatino, was numbered. Giovanni Palatino's *Libro nuovo d'imparare a scrivera* was published in Rome in 1540 and became one of the most used, wide-ranging writing manuals of the sixteenth century. Zapf was an apt student of the European masters, and contemporary *Palatino* is one of his contributions to modern typography.

Substantive Editing:
Michael S. Hyatt

Copy Editing:
Susan Kirby

Cover Design:
Steve Diggs & Friends
Nashville, Tennessee

Page Composition:
Xerox Ventura Publisher
Printware 720 IQ Laser Printer

Printing and Binding:
Maple-Vail Printing Group
York, Pennsylvania

Cover Printing:
Strine Printing
York, Pennsylvania